Simply Understanding
the New Testament

Simply Understanding the New Testament

Irving L. Jensen

World Wide Publications
A ministry of the Billy Graham Evangelistic Association
1303 Hennepin Avenue, Minneapolis, Minnesota 55403

Simply Understanding the New Testament
by Dr. Irving L. Jensen

Copyright © 1988 Dr. Irving L. Jensen.

World Wide Publications is the publishing ministry of the Billy Graham
Evangelistic Association.

Scripture quotations in this publication are from the HOLY BIBLE, NEW
INTERNATIONAL VERSION. Copyright © 1973, 1978, 1984 International
Bible Society. Used by permission of Zondervan Bible Publishers.

The chart on page 26 is reprinted by permission from Dr. Irving L. Jensen,
Survey of the New Testament (Chicago: Moody Press, 1981), 202.

Library of Congress Catalog Card Number: 88-50835

ISBN # 0-89066-116-2

Printed in the United States of America.

CONTENTS

READING AND STUDYING THE NEW TESTAMENT

The last words God ever wrote to man are in the pages of the New Testament. The Book is that important and precious. It offers eternal life to all sinners, and spiritual food for Christians growing in the Lord. Where would the world be today if we did not have the truth in such verses as John 3:16?

A Miracle Book

The very existence of the Bible is a miracle. God breathed upon chosen writers (2 Timothy 3:16) and these "men spoke from God as they were carried along by the Holy Spirit" (2 Peter 1:21). The result was a holy library of books, whose words are trustworthy and perfect.

The Bible is a miracle because of the way all sixty-six books became two parts, now called the Old Testament and the New Testament. Centuries after the books were written, God gave his people, the church, the spiritual understanding to know which books he had inspired. These, and no other books, make up the two testaments of God's Book, the Bible. The Old Testament has thirty-nine books; the New Testament has twenty-seven books. The order of the New Testament books, as they appear in our Bibles today, is the work of the early church.

The Bible is a miracle book because it has lasted through centuries of copying, translating, and attacks by enemies of God. The Bible's message and unity make it a miracle book. It was written by about forty authors, over a period of 2,000 years, but it is *one Book*. The New Testament continues and fulfills God's message in the Old Testament. Christianity didn't just happen. God had been working among the people of the world, especially Israel, for many centuries before Christ. Then, "when the time had fully come, God sent his Son" (Galatians 4:4). The rest of the story is the message of the New Testament. The Old Testament is the promise; the New Testament fulfills that promise.

Key Truths of the New Testament
There are key truths underlying all the details of the New Testament text. We find these truths constantly reappearing as we study the New Testament books:

1. Sin is man's basic, desperate problem.
2. Christ's payment for sin is the heart of the gospel.
3. The human race has no hope outside of God's grace.
4. The gospel is God's message to the whole world.
5. The *work* of Christ depends on the *person* of Christ.
6. The main reason for miracles is to show Christ, the Miracle Worker.
7. The Holy Spirit is actively working in this age.
8. All world history moves toward the last days.
9. The final event of history will be when God places Jesus Christ on the throne as ruler over all (Philippians 2:9-11).
10. The New Testament gives God's full directions for living a life that is pleasing to him.

HINTS FOR READING AND STUDYING THE NEW TESTAMENT

Everyone should read and study the Bible, because God gave the Bible to everyone. It is a long book, but we have a lifetime to read it. Each time we read, difficult sections become clearer, and the important truths stand out even more. Bible reading is truly exciting and enjoyable.

How can we get the most out of our Bible reading? The answer is, by *studying* the Bible text as we read it. Our starting point for studying is reading and thinking about what we have read.

One Purpose
The basic purpose of Bible study is to learn what God wants to teach us. We should always keep in mind: *This is from God to us* (Hebrews 1:2). Then we look to the Holy Spirit for his help in understanding.

Two Stages
There are two stages in studying a book or passage of the Bible.

First we look at the whole (*survey*), then we examine the parts
(*analysis*). Most of the study suggestions in this book are about
the survey stage.

Three Activities in Analysis (examining the parts)

When we analyze a passage (whether it is a chapter or segment
or paragraph), we first see what the text says (*observation*), then
we find out what it means (*interpretation*), then we arrive at ways
to apply the text to our lives (*application*). Since observation is
basic to everything else we should spend much of our time
observing. Usually the surrounding sentences are our best help
for finding the *meaning* (interpretation).

Four Uses of the Pencil

"The pencil is one of the best eyes for seeing." Writing notes in
a book is a big help, because it keeps us wide awake; it puts into
words our own thinking; it opens doors to other discoveries; it
helps us remember what we are seeing. Here are some useful
ways to use your pencil in Bible study:

1. Mark the Bible text to show *emphases* (main points) and
relations (how it fits with other passages). These are the best
clues to what the passage is saying. For example, if a word
is repeated often in a paragraph, we can underline each
appearance. Or, if we see a phrase at the beginning of a
paragraph and then see a similar thought put into words
at the end, we may show this *relation* by drawing a line
between the two.

2. Make paragraphs stand out. It helps to set off paragraphs
by drawing lines between them. We can also write the outline
points of the book at their appropriate places in the Bible
text. We can write short notes in the margins that say clearly
what we learned from the paragraph.

3. Write notes in a notebook for a permanent record. The
notes should be short and clear, highlighting words and
phrases of the Bible text.

4. Print on a separate paper a "talking text" of verses and
paragraphs. A talking text is our own words and phrases that
make the text *talk*— especially the *emphasized* parts and the

related parts. It is an excellent way to put ourselves into the text. Key words and phrases stand out sharply. (See example below).

TALKING TEXT of Romans 15:17-19a

17   So I am proud of
            what I have DONE for GOD
                    in CHRIST JESUS.

18   → I will not talk about
            anything I DID MYSELF.
       → I will talk only about
            what CHRIST has DONE with me
        in LEADING the non-Jewish people
                    to OBEY GOD.
            They have OBEYED GOD
          ① because of what I have said and DONE.
19a   And they have OBEYED GOD
          ② because of 1) the power of MIRACLES
                    and 2) the great things they saw,
                    and 3) the power of the HOLY SPIRIT.

HOW TO READ THE NEW TESTAMENT BOOKS IN TOPICAL ORDER

There are different orders we might follow in reading the twenty-seven books of the New Testament. Three of these are:

1. *Canonical Order.* This is the order we find in our Bibles. It begins with the four Gospels and Acts (history), then is followed by letters (interpretation), and ends with Revelation (Prophecy).

2. *Chronological Order.* This is the order based on *when* the books were written.

3. *Topical Order.* This is by groups of similar subjects. For example, books stressing end times appear in a last group. Below is one suggested order. You will see that one of the four Gospels heads each group. The value of this order is *variety* (for example, you are not reading the four Gospels together).

Topical Order of Reading the New Testament

1. *Old Testament Connections:*
   Matthew
   Hebrews
   James
2. *Church Beginnings:*
   Luke
   Acts
   Romans
   1 Corinthians
   2 Corinthians
3. *Church Growing:*
   Mark
   Galatians
   Ephesians
   Philippians
   Colossians
   Philemon
   1 Timothy
   Titus
   2 Timothy
4. *Last Days:*
   John
   1 John
   2 John
   3 John
   1 Thessalonians
   2 Thessalonians
   1 Peter
   2 Peter
   Jude
   Revelation

DESCRIPTIONS AND STUDY GUIDES FOR NEW TESTAMENT BOOKS

On the following pages you will find a brief description of each New Testament book, and a guide to aid your study of that book. First, each book is described by its:

Setting
Author
First Readers
Place and Date Written
Purpose
Theme
Key Words
Outline
Key Verses

This information will help you understand the historical setting, topics and problems being discussed. The outlines will show you how the author develops the book's theme.

Following the description and outline is a section to help you
read and study the Bible text. Since we learn most by our own
personal study, the helps given are to encourage your indepen-
dent work. Following is a brief explanation of some of the helps
you will find:

Scanning
Scanning means looking at the Bible text part by part or segment by segment. In most modern Bible translations, a "segment" is a group of paragraphs under one title. For example, in
the New International Version, the segment Romans 5:1-11 has
three paragraphs, and its title is, "Peace and Joy."

Overview
This part of the guides helps you go into more detail concerning
the outline and topics of the book.

Important Passages
These passages are noted to help you focus on main sections of
the Bible text. The entire Bible is important, but some passages
have special significance.

MATTHEW

Jesus and His Promised Kingdom

Setting
While we study the books of the New Testament, it helps to picture ourselves living back in the first century, when the books
were written. Matthew is a good place to begin studying the New
Testament, because it ties together the Old and New Testaments.

Many religious Jews of the first century wanted to know if Jesus
was truly the Messiah—the Anointed One, the Christ—foretold
in the Old Testament. They had studied their Hebrew Scriptures
with their foretelling of a new kingdom to come, and now they
had the opportunity to read what the Jewish writer Matthew
had to say. He often quoted the Old Testament. We can imagine
their joy and excitement to read in Matthew over and over again
that things were "just as the prophets wrote."

Author
The author is Matthew, a Jewish tax collector who became a
disciple of Jesus (10:3).

First Readers
Matthew especially wrote to the Jews, but he also had non-Jews in mind.

Date Written
Matthew wrote possibly in the late fifties or sixties A.D., before the destruction of Jerusalem in A.D. 70.

Purpose
Matthew's main purpose was to show his Jewish readers that Jesus is king of God's promised kingdom.

Theme
Jesus is king of God's promised kingdom.

Key Words
Kingdom, fulfilled, righteous, worship, Father.

Outline
Jesus and His Promised Kingdom
   A. Birth and preparation of the king 1:1-4:11
   B. Message and ministry of the king 4:12-16:20
   C. The king's death and resurrection 16:21-28:20

Key Verses
"Where is the one who has been born king of the Jews? We saw his star in the east and have come to worship him" (2:2).

"Therefore go and make disciples of all nations, baptizing them in the name of the Father and of the Son and of the Holy Spirit" (28:19).

STUDYING THE TEXT OF MATTHEW

Scanning
Looking at the Bible text, we first survey the whole book, noting such things as general make-up, highlights, key words and turning points.

Beginning and End

The opening and closing of a book may reveal something about its purpose. In the opening verse we see three names: Jesus Christ, David and Abraham. These are important names in Jewish history. In the closing verses (28:19,20), notice the words "all nations" and "world." This is important, because Matthew has been writing mainly to Jewish readers about the Jews' Messiah. But now they are to share this Messiah with the whole world.

Important Passages

Most of the text of Matthew is a story line, or *narrative*, followed by Jesus' teachings, or *discourse*. This arrangement appears five times. Each teaching section closes with the statement, "When Jesus had finished saying these things," or a similar statement.

Here is a list of the five teaching sections. If we read these now, we'll have a good understanding of Jesus' teaching ministry.

Sermon on the Mount.....................Chapters 5-7
Instructions for the Twelve Apostles........Chapter 10
Stories About the Kingdom...............Chapter 13
Life in the Kingdom....................Chapter 18
End of the Age.......................Chapters 24,25

Overview

The book of Matthew breaks into three main parts:

1:1 PRESENTATION	4:12 PROCLAMATION	16:21 PASSION 28:20

Presentation (1:1-4:11). These chapters show how Jesus was presented to the world.

Proclamation (4:12-16:20). We see the opening of Jesus' public ministry in verse 4:12. We learn of Jesus' main activity during this period in 4:17—"From that time on Jesus began to preach." That is why the middle section of the overview is called proclamation. Three of Jesus' five teaching sessions are reported in this section. Among these are Jesus' stories called parables (chapter 13), his favorite way of teaching. As we read these chapters we

can learn much about who Jesus is and what Jesus considers
important for us.

Passion, or Sufferings of Christ (16:21-28:20). The opening verse
tells us that a new section is coming up: "From that time on
Jesus began to explain to his disciples that he must go to
Jerusalem" (16:21). In the last part of that verse Jesus tells what
will happen to him in Jerusalem. He will suffer, be killed, and
be raised from death on the third day. The three parts of this
section are Jesus' final ministries (chapters 19-23); his teachings
on the end times (chapters 24,25); and his death and resurrection (chapters 26-28).

After reading the segment headings, read the full Bible text of
this heart-moving account of Jesus' life.

If studying the New Testament in topical order,
go now to Hebrews.

MARK

The Servant Jesus

Setting

Jesus' public ministry involved traveling from place to place, so he was grateful for the kindness of friends for meals and bed. While in Jerusalem he may have been a house guest of a lady called Mary, who opened her house to believers (see Acts 12:12-17). Young John Mark, usually called Mark, could have been this Mary's son. As a teenager he surely must have been attracted to this special guest. This is the Mark whom God prepared to write one of the four Gospels. Mark wasn't called to be one of Jesus' twelve disciples, but he became a close friend of the disciple Peter. It was from Peter's first-hand reports of Jesus' ministry that Mark wrote his Gospel.

Author

The writer of this second Gospel was John Mark, son of Mary (Acts 12:12) and cousin of Barnabas. The eight New Testament references to Mark show him to be an active servant of Christ.

First Readers
Mark wrote for Gentile readers in general and Romans in particular. The Roman mind was impressed more by action and power than by preaching and talk. Mark's natural style was to write an active, fast-paced Gospel.

Date Written
There are various views as to date, from early, 50-64, to late, 65-70 A.D. Many scholars believe that the book of Mark was the first of the four Gospels to be written.

Purpose
Mark stresses the *actions* more than the *words* of Jesus.

Theme
Jesus came to give his life as a sacrifice to save people.

Key Words
Serve, save, then (meaning "immediately").

Outline
The Servant Jesus
   A. Service of Jesus 1:1-9:1
   B. Sacrifice of Jesus 9:2-15:47
   C. Triumph of Jesus 16:1-20

Key Verse.
"For even the Son of Man did not come to be served, but to serve, and to give his life as a ransom for many" (10:45).

STUDYING THE TEXT OF MARK

Scanning
To get a feel for the book, turn the pages again and read each segment title (if your Bible has them) and its first verse. Before long you will begin to sense that Mark is a book more of action than of talking.

Beginning and End
This would be a good time to compare the opening verse with

the closing verses of the book. Why does Mark open with the words, "This is the beginning of the gospel" (1:1)? What is happening to the gospel in the last two verses of the book?

Overview
The book of Mark, like the other three Gospels, is the story of selected parts of Jesus' life. Mark's account emphasizes a key turning point in Jesus' life. Read 8:27-30 now and look for key words and phrases.

Here is the story setting: Jesus and his disciples have come to the northern city of Caesarea Philippi. Up until this time, Jesus has shown who he is by the miracles he did. But he has not yet plainly told the people or his disciples what would happen to him in Jerusalem.

Next he asks questions about himself: "Who do people say I am?" and "Who do *you* say I am?" Peter answers correctly: "You are the Christ" (8:27-29).

It is then that Jesus begins to reveal his coming death and resurrection to life again. Mark says Jesus told them plainly what would happen (8:32). The story of Mark from this point on is the story of sacrifice. Jesus begins the journey to Jerusalem, stating again and again that he is the Christ.

Key Outline
Jesus Shows Who He Is Through Serving	(1:1-8:26)
Who Am I?	(8:27-30)
Jesus Proves Who He Is Through Sacrifice	(8:31-16:20)

KEY OUTLINE OF MARK

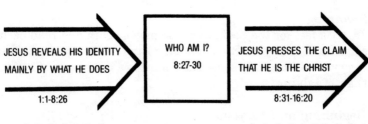

Now is a good time to read the whole book of Mark, section by section. As we read the first section (1:1-8:26)—*Jesus shows who he is through serving*—we want to see how Jesus tried to identify himself as the promised Messiah sent from God the Father. Then the middle section (8:27-30) asks the question: *Who am I?* The last section (8:31-16:20) *proves who he is*—the Messiah who will save us from our sins—through his sacrifice.

It will help us to read these last chapters with this outline in mind:

Jesus as Redeemer	(to buy back)	8:31-10:52
Jesus as Lord	(the ruler over all)	11:1-13:37
Jesus as Sacrifice	(to give up his life)	14:1-15:47
Jesus as Victor	(to win over death, sin and the devil)	16:1-20

If studying the New Testament in topical order, go now to Galatians.

LUKE

The Son of Man Among Men

Setting

For many years after Jesus went up to heaven, the world did not have the gospel in any complete, God-inspired book. Then in God's timing men inspired by the Holy Spirit wrote the Gospels for permanent record. When we compare the messages of the four accounts, we see likenesses and differences, all of them perfectly telling God's good news. The chart on the next page compares Luke with the other Gospels.

Author

The third Gospel was written by Luke, a Greek Christian and medical doctor (Colossians 4:14). Luke, like Mark, was not a disciple of Jesus during his earthly ministry. While living in Antioch he may have been converted under the ministry of Paul (see Acts 11:25,26). Luke is a kind and humble man of prayer with a sympathetic heart for all people in need.

COMPARISON OF THE FOUR GOSPELS

	MATTHEW	MARK	LUKE	JOHN
Jesus as:	King of Israel	Servant of the Lord	Son of Man	Son of God
Reader:	Jew	Roman	Greek	World
Prominent Ideas	Law and Promise	Power and Service	Grace and Fellowship	Glory and Life

First Readers
The intended readers are Theophilus, a friend of Luke, Gentiles and people everywhere.

Date Written
Around A.D. 60, at the end of Paul's missionary journeys.

Purpose
Luke's purpose is to give an orderly, true report of the life of Jesus (1:1-4).

Theme
Jesus, the Son of Man, loves sinners and offers everyone God's salvation.

Key Words
Son of Man, love, sinners, praise.

Outline
The Son of Man Among Men
  A. Preparation 1:1-4:13
  B. Signs 4:14-9:50
  C. Teaching 9:51-19:27
  D. Sacrifice 19:28-24:53

Key Verse
"For the Son of Man came to seek and to save what was lost"
(19:10).

STUDYING THE TEXT OF LUKE

Scanning
By now we have learned methods that quickly and easily give us the "feel" of the book we are about to read and study. When we turn the pages of Luke, we see that the account is long—in fact, Luke is the longest book of the New Testament. (Matthew has more chapters, but Luke contains more writing.)

Beginning and End
When we first look at chapter 1, we are surprised that the main person in the story is not Jesus but John, son of Elizabeth. But all of chapter 1 really is looking forward to the Savior. John's ministry was to "make ready a people prepared for the coming of the Lord" (1:17). He was Jesus' forerunner. Then, in chapter 2, comes the great moment. Mary gives birth to her first son (2:7).

Chapter 1 praises God joyfully in the songs of Mary (1:46-55) and Zechariah (1:67-79). And in the closing verses of Luke we find joy and happiness, with the happy followers of Jesus praising God in the temple all the time (24:50-53). This atmosphere of joy will appear from time to time as we read and study Luke's Gospel.

Overview
The *words* and *works* of Jesus are the two subjects Luke writes about. In his second book, Acts, he says that his first scroll, Luke, was "about all that Jesus began to do and teach" (Acts 1:1). At the end of the gospel account two men walking to Emmaus declare that Jesus was "powerful in word and deed" (24:19).

The following are the four main sections of the book:

LUKE: SON OF MAN AMONG MEN

1:1 PREPARATION	4:14 IDENTIFICATION	9:51 INSTRUCTION	19:28 SACRIFICE 24:53
	miracles abound here —what Jesus DID	stories abound here —what Jesus SAID	

Preparation (1:1-4:13). This is about getting the people ready for

Jesus' coming, through John's ministry, and Jesus' preparing for his public ministry.

Signs (4:14-9:50). Jesus wanted to convince the people that he was the Messiah—the *Son of God* coming with great power and the *Son of Man* with concern for lost sinners. Look for signs of his power and love.

Teaching (9:51-19:27). This section is filled with the stories (parables) of Jesus. He wanted the people to see that the Son of Man came to find lost people and save them (19:10). It hurts us to see his love rejected. "All the people saw this and began to mutter, 'He has gone to be the guest of a sinner' " (19:7).

Sacrifice (19:28-24:53). All the Gospels close on the moving themes of Jesus' death and coming back to life, and his last words. Read these chapters slowly, thinking carefully about these great truths.

*If studying the New Testament in topical order,
go now to Acts.*

JOHN

Life in Jesus, the Son of God

Setting

When the Apostle John wrote his Gospel, many years had passed since the other three accounts had been written. Matthew's Gospel had been written mainly to Jews, Mark's to the Romans, and Luke's to the Gentiles. John's is for everyone.

During these years the church has been thinking more about the meaning of Jesus' mission and teachings. That partly explains why the Holy Spirit inspires and guides John to include more explanations in Jesus' own words in this final Gospel account.

Author

John, the disciple of Jesus and brother of the disciple James, is believed to be the author. John was a fisherman when Jesus called him to be his disciple (Mark 1:19,20). He was a close friend of Peter and later became a leader of the Jerusalem church (Galatians 2:9). John was a man of courage, loyalty and love. His love for Jesus and people shines forth in this Gospel and also in his letters that follow.

First Readers
While John is writing this Gospel, he pictures everybody, Jew and Gentile, as his readers. Unbelievers are especially on his mind.

Date Written
John wrote this Gospel during the last years of his life, around A.D. 85. Soon after that he wrote three letters and the book of Revelation.

Purpose
John wanted to win unbelievers to a saving faith in Christ and also to strengthen believers in their faith (20:30,31).

Theme
For eternal life, believe in Jesus as the Savior sent by God.

Key Words
Believe is used ninety-eight times; and another important word is *love*.

Outline
Life in Jesus, the Son of God
Public Ministry 1:1-12:36a
  A. Time of Jesus begins 1:1-4:54
  B. Years of conflict 5:1-12:36a
Private Ministry 12:36b-21:25
  A. Day of preparation 12:36b-17:26
  B. Hour of sacrifice 18:1-19:42
  C. Dawn of victory 20:1-21:25

Key Verses
"Jesus did many other miraculous signs in the presence of his disciples, which are not recorded in this book. But these are written that you may believe that Jesus is the Christ, the Son of God, and that by believing you may have life in his name" (John 20:30,31).

STUDYING THE TEXT OF JOHN

Scanning
First scan the twenty-one chapters of John by reading the segment titles. Then go back and scan the opening paragraph of each chapter.

Beginning and End
John's Gospel is enclosed by an introduction (1:1-18) and conclusion (21:1-25). The introduction sets the tone for the book, and is the finest short gospel message in the Bible. It is an excellent passage to memorize.

The story line or narrative begins at 1:19, after the introduction. Then 20:30,31 show us how the story line ends.

Overview
John's narrative is in two parts: Public and private ministry.

1:1 PUBLIC MINISTRY (3 years)		12:36b PRIVATE MINISTRY (few days) 21:25	
introductions to the people	5:1 opposition by the rulers	introductions for the disciples	18:1 crises and triumph

Turning Point
The turning point from public to private ministry is in the last sentence of 12:36: "When he had finished speaking, Jesus left and hid himself from them." Up to this point Jesus has been sharing the good news of salvation with everyone, but most have rejected him. Now, looking ahead to the cross, he begins to give last instructions to his disciples.

Important Passages
Now read the main sections of John, picturing how each part fits into the whole book.

Introduction (1:1-18)

Jesus Meets With Nicodemus (3:1-21)

Farewell Talk (14:1-16:33)

Jesus Prays for All Believers: The Highly Priestly Prayer (17:1-26). This is the most moving prayer of the Bible. If we want to feel the heart throb of Jesus, here is the place to spend much reading and thought.

Jesus Dies on the Cross: The Crucifixion (18:1-19:42)

Jesus Rises From the Dead: The Resurrection (20:1-31)

After we have read these important passages, we can go back and read the other chapters. And it won't take us long to see that all of John is very important.

If studying the New Testament in topical order,
go now to 1 John.

ACTS

The Beginnings of the Christian Church

Setting

Acts follows the Gospels and is background to the letters that follow. If Christ had not risen from the grave, there would be no book of Acts.

RELATION OF ACTS TO THE GOSPELS

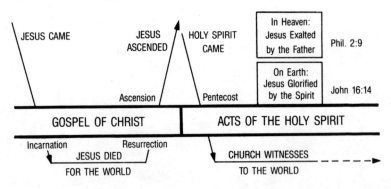

Two main areas of attention in the New Testament are the Holy
Spirit, and those who make up the church, the Body of Christ:
1) The four Gospels present Christ as the Foundation and Head
of that church; 2) Acts records the beginning and early history
of the church; 3) The twenty-one letters or epistles offer teaching
for the church; and 4) The book of Revelation prophesies end
times and the endless reign of Christ with his church.

Author
When we compare Luke 1:1-4 and Acts 1:1 we see why Luke,
though unnamed, is regarded as the author of Acts.

First Readers
Acts is addressed to the author's friend, Theophilus. Luke also
wanted Christian believers everywhere to learn how the church
grew, and he wanted the unbelieving world to see how the
believers triumphed even through persecution.

Date Written
Around A.D. 61, near the end of Paul's Roman imprisonment
(chapter 28).

Purposes
To show how Jesus Christ started the Christian church, to record
its amazing growth and to help believers grow in Christian life
and service.

Theme
Christians are Christ's witnesses of the good news to the whole
world.

Key Words
Witness, preach, boldly, Jews, Greeks.

Outline
The Beginnings of the Christian Church
Jerusalem
   A. The church is born 1:1-2:47
   B. The church grows through testing 3:1-8:1a
Judea and Samaria 8:1b-12:25
   A. The church is scattered 8:1b-9:31
   B. The church includes Gentiles 9:32-12:25

Every Part of the World 13:1-28:31
   A. The church extends overseas 13:1-21:17
   B. The church's leader on trial 21:18-28:31

Key Verse.

"But you will receive power when the Holy Spirit comes on you; and you will be my witnesses in Jerusalem, and in all Judea and Samaria, and to the ends of the earth" (1:8).

STUDYING THE TEXT OF ACTS

Scanning

First we scan Acts. This includes reading the segment headings and the first verses of each chapter. We observe that Acts has 28 chapters, the same number as Matthew.

Beginning and End

Read the first paragraph again (1:1-5), noting how it links Acts with Luke. Something new appears—words about fulfillment of a promise (1:4). This promise is recorded in John 14:26. Go back and read that verse. Now in Acts 1:5 we learn that the Holy Spirit is that gift.

The last verse of Acts shows something interesting: No one tries to stop Paul from speaking about Jesus. He was unhindered! Is this an example of the Spirit's ministry through believers, spoken about by Jesus in 1:5?

Overview

A good starting point for getting an overview of the whole book of Acts is the key verse: " . . . you will be my witnesses in Jerusalem, and in all Judea and Samaria, and to the ends of the earth" (1:8b). We can see on the maps how the order of these names suggests an expanding area. The good news would be preached first in Jerusalem and eventually to the whole world. This is exactly what happened.

ACTS: BEGINNINGS OF THE CHRISTIAN CHURCH

1:1 JERUSALEM	8:1b JUDEA and SAMARIA	13:1	EVERY PART OF THE WORLD	28:31
CHURCH BORN AND TESTED	CHURCH SCATTERED	CHURCH EXTENDED		
JEWISH PERIOD	TRANSITION	UNIVERSAL GOSPEL		

There were also two other progressions during these years:

1) The church was born and grew through testing (1:1-8:1a); it was scattered by persecutions (8:1b-12:25) and it reached the ends of the earth (13:1-28:31).

2) Almost all believers of the first local churches were Jews (1:1-8:1a); the apostles soon began to preach that the good news was also for Gentiles (8:1b-12:25); and eventually the church's message was recognized as a universal gospel—for everyone (13:1-28:31).

Important Passages
With the overview in mind, this is a good time to read some of the prominent passages of Acts. Then we can return and read the rest of the chapters.

The church is born 2:10-47
Stephen's life and death 6:1-8:1a
Saul's conversion 9:1-19a
The church includes Gentiles 9:32-12:25
Paul the missionary 13:1-21:17
Paul the prisoner 21:18-28:31

For twenty centuries the Lord has not been without loyal witnesses, compelled by the Holy Spirit to share the good news of Jesus with all the world. Are we among this number?

If studying the New Testament in topical order,
go now to Romans.

ROMANS

God's Salvation for Sinners

Setting
The problems in the world today are the result of the sinfulness of man. Hope for the future cannot come through people. It must come from a good, all-powerful, and loving God. God inspired a man to write Romans to tell the world that there *is hope* of eternal salvation for everyone who believes in Jesus.

Author
The opening verse identifies Paul as the author, a servant of Christ Jesus and a chosen apostle of God to be "set apart for the gospel" (1:1).

Paul was born of Jewish parents around the time of Christ's birth. He was raised as a strict Pharisee and became a leader of zealous Jews who wanted to kill the Christians (read Acts 26:4-11). His conversion to Christ came while traveling to Damascus to try to stop the spread of Christianity (Acts 9:1-19a).

In A.D. 47 Paul went on his first missionary journey. Twenty years later he died in Rome as a Christian martyr.

First Readers
Paul wrote to Christians in Rome, a mixed fellowship of Jews and Gentiles gathering in various homes and meeting places. He knew many of them from past contacts, but he had not yet visited the city (1:13).

Date Written
Paul wrote this letter from Corinth around A.D. 56, toward the end of his third missionary journey (Acts 18:23-21:17).

Purposes
Paul gave instruction regarding basic truths of salvation: how to become a Christian and how to live the Christian life.

Theme
God's righteousness is given to the sinner who believes in Christ Jesus.

Key Words
Sin, law, righteousness, death, flesh, faith, believe, all, Spirit.

Outline
God's Salvation for Sinners
Prologue 1:1-17
Doctrine 1:18-11:36
   A. God's holiness in condemning sin 1:18-3:20
   B. God's grace in making sinners right 3:21-5:21
   C. God's power in making believers holy 6:1-8:39
   D. God's design in saving Jew and Gentile 9:1-11:36
Practice 12:1-15:13
   A. The Christian servant 12:1-21
   B. The Christian citizen 13:1-14
   C. The Christian brother 14:1-15:13
Epilogue 15:14-16:27

Key Verses.
"I am not ashamed of the gospel, because it is the power of God for the salvation of everyone who believes: first for the Jew, then for the Gentile. For in the gospel a righteousness from God is

revealed, a righteousness that is by faith from first to last"
(1:16,17a).

STUDYING THE TEXT OF ROMANS

Scanning
Romans has sixteen chapters. As we thumb through all the
pages, the segment titles reveal that Romans is about interesting
and key subjects.

Beginning and End
The first seventeen verses of the book, called a *prologue*, are
Paul's greeting and introduction to the whole book (1:1-17). Let's
read this warm *prologue* now. Then go to the end of the book
and read the concluding epilogue, which is made up of personal
messages (15:14-33) and blessings (16:1-27). We can't help but
feel Paul's excitement and joy as he wrote.

When we compare the beginning and end of the letter, we get
a feeling of victory and fulfillment. For example, near the beginning Paul wrote a warm note of gratitude: "I thank my God
through Jesus Christ for all of you" (1:8), and his last line is one
of loud praise: "To the only wise God be glory forever through
Jesus Christ! Amen" (16:27).

Overview
The letter has two main parts: Paul first teaches Bible truths,
called doctrine (1:18-11:36); then he tells the believers how to
apply that doctrine to their lives (12:1-15:13). Note in 11:36 that
the word "Amen" ends the doctrinal section and "Therefore"
(12:1) begins the following practical section.

An easy outline for remembering the five subjects in order is:
sin, salvation, sanctification, sovereignty and service.

ROMANS: GOD'S SALVATION FOR SINNERS

DOCTRINAL			"Amen"	"So" PRACTICAL
1:18 SIN	3:21 SALVATION	6:1 SANCTI-FICATION	9:1 SOVEREIGNTY	12:1 SERVICE 15:13
GOD'S HOLINESS	GOD'S GRACE	GOD'S POWER	GOD'S SOVEREIGNTY	GOD'S GLORY

Further Reading

Now we can read the Bible text of the five sections, referring to the outline as we read. It should not surprise us to see God's part (for example, his holiness in 1:18-3:20) in every part of salvation:

1:18-3:20 *Need of Salvation*—We are sinners, God is holy.

3:21-5:21 *Way of Salvation*—We are saved by God's grace, through faith.

6:1-8:39 *Life of Salvation*—God gives power to live the Christian life.

9:1-11:36 *Scope of Salvation*—God saves believing Jews and Gentiles.

12:1-15:13 *Service of Salvation*—We are saved to serve God, for his glory.

Important Passages.

The main passages of Romans explain why one Bible student has said, "A thorough study of this epistle is really a theological education in itself." It would be very helpful for us to read these passages over and over again!

The whole world condemned (1:18-3:20)
Justification (making "right") (3:21-5:21)
Sanctification (making "holy") (6:1-8:39)
Israel (past, chapter 9; present, chapter 10;
   future, chapter 11)
Christian conduct (12:1-15:13)

If studying the New Testament in topical order, go now to 1 Corinthians.

1 CORINTHIANS

Problems of a Local Church

Setting
1 Corinthians is a letter about problems of Christians in a local church, especially in their relationships with one another. Paul visited and preached in Corinth, the business center of Greece, on his second missionary journey (Acts 17:15-18:18). The new Christian converts from that trip started a local church. Then, five years later, Paul wrote 1 Corinthians to help them with problems that had come up. He wrote from a broken heart, but with the faith they would repent and God would heal their church.

Author
Paul was the writer, and Sosthenes was his helper (see Acts 18:17).

First Readers
Paul wrote to the young converts of "the church of God in Corinth, to those sanctified in Christ Jesus" (1:2). Their position in Christ is *holiness* because they have believed the good news

of salvation. But they are guilty of sins which are tearing down the church.

Date Written
About A.D. 55, toward the end of Paul's third missionary journey.

Purposes
Among Paul's purposes were these: to correct false teaching; to help the believers see their sins and weaknesses and to encourage them in how to have a healthy, maturing Christian life.

Theme
Jesus Christ and the Holy Spirit answer all the spiritual problems of Christians and the local churches where they worship and fellowship.

Key Words
Resurrection, cross, in Christ Jesus, Spirit, love, body, gifts, wisdom.

Outline
Problems of a Local Church
Introduction 1:1-9
Bad Reports 1:10-6:20
  A. Divisions 1:10-4:21
  B. Disorders 5:1-6:20
Answering Questions 7:1-15:58
  A. Personal problems 7:1-11:1
  B. Public worship problems 11:2-14:40
  C. Questions about the resurrection body 15:1-58
Conclusion 16:1-24

Key Verses
"But thanks be to God! He gives us the victory through our Lord Jesus Christ. Therefore, my dear brothers, stand firm. Let nothing move you. Always give yourselves fully to the work of the Lord, because you know that your labor in the Lord is not in vain" (1 Corinthians 15:57,58).

STUDYING THE TEXT OF 1 CORINTHIANS

Scanning
Turning the pages of the sixteen chapters and reading the segment titles will give a feel for the whole letter.

Beginning and End
Now we can read the introduction (1:1-9), keeping in mind as we read these lines that Paul was about to write some severe criticisms of the people's sins. When we read the last chapter (16) we'll see that Paul didn't want to say "good-bye" on a sad note.

Overview
Paul wrote the letter in response to two things: a) reports being spread about the church's problems (1:11); and b) questions the Corinthians had asked about personal and worship service problems (see 7:1 "The matters you wrote about"). From this we conclude that there are two main sections in the letter: bad reports (1:10-6:20) and answering questions (7:1-15:58).

Now we can go back and read each segment to learn what those reports and inquiries were about.

1 CORINTHIANS: PROBLEMS OF A LOCAL CHURCH

INTRODUCTION 1:1-9	ACKNOWLEDGING REPORTS		ANSWERING INQUIRIES			CONCLUSION 16:1-24
	problems of the congregation		personal problems	worship service problems		
	DISUNITY	DEPRAVITIES	MARRIAGE	CHRISTIAN LIBERTY	ORDER, SPIRITUAL GIFTS AND RESURRECTION	
	1:10	5:1	7:1	8:1	11:2 15:58	

Problems in the Church at Corinth. We look for *answers* when we read about the problems:

1. *Not Getting Along Together* (1:10-4:21). "I beg that all of you agree with one another" (see 1:10).

2. *Disorders* (5:1-6:20). Paul writes about carelessness (5:1-13); lawsuits (6:1-11); and immorality (6:12-20).

3. *Marriage* (7:1-40). Paul answers questions about marriage, widows being single, and sexual sin.

4. *Christian Freedom* (8:1-11:1). We learn from these passages how to apply Christian principles to questionable practices today.

5. *Public Worship* (11:2-14:40). The place of women and men (11:2-16); the Lord's Supper (11:17-34); and spiritual gifts (12:1-14:40).

6. *The Resurrection Body* (15:1-58). This is the key chapter of 1 Corinthians. The Corinthians had two questions about the resurrection, and Paul gave full answers to both: "Will people be raised from the dead?" (15:12); and "What kind of body will they have?" (15:35).

Answers to the Problems. There are no problems in 1 Corinthians without answers, which makes the letter so valuable. The resurrected Christ and the powerful Holy Spirit are the answers to the problems. In chapter 15, verses such as 1,2,49,56 and 58 will stay with us to help us long after we have finished reading the letter.

> *If studying the New Testament in topical order,*
> *go now to 2 Corinthians.*

2 CORINTHIANS

Gospel Ministry and God's Gifts

Setting

Paul's two letters to the Corinthians are about problems we meet when telling of the good news. Happily, these letters say much about answers to all problems. In 1 Corinthians the problems are mainly those of a local church. In 2 Corinthians the same church is involved, but most of the discussion concerns Paul's personal problem of making his Corinthian friends believe he is a true apostle of Christ and is preaching the true gospel. In the opening verse of the letter he speaks to the problem and points to its solution: "I am an apostle of Christ Jesus . . . because that is what God wanted" (see 1:1).

Two marks of a mature, healthy Christian are beliefs based on the truth, and total commitment to Christ. By studying 2 Corinthians we'll see what it means to be a good witness for Christ.

Author

The writer is Paul, who wrote 1 Corinthians and also other let-

ters, many of which are in the New Testament. His helper
Timothy sends along greetings.

First Readers
Paul wrote to the same Christians he addressed in 1 Corinthians.
They still needed spiritual help, which Paul offered through this
follow-up letter and another personal visit (12:14,13:1).

Date Written
A.D. 56. Paul was in Macedonia, on his way to Corinth.

Purposes
Among Paul's main purposes in writing were these: to teach and
advise about the Christian life; to defend himself because of
criticism by people in the church (see 10:10; 13:3); and to give
further instruction about an offering for the poor believers in
Jerusalem (9:1-5; also see 1 Corinthians 16:3).

Theme
God gave us this work—to tell everyone that Jesus Christ is Lord
(4:1,5).

Key Words
Sorrow, glory, suffering, serve, comfort.

Outline
  Gospel Ministry and God's Gifts
  Greeting 1:1,2
    A. Sketch of Paul's ministry 1:3-7:16
    B. Appeal about giving 8:1-9:15
    C. Defense of Paul's ministry 10:1-13:10
  Farewell 13:11-14

Key Verses
*"We are therefore Christ's ambassadors, as though God were mak-
ing his appeal through us. We implore you on Christ's behalf: Be
reconciled to God. God made him who had no sin to be sin for
us, so that in him we might become the righteousness of God."
(2 Corinthians 5:20,21).*

STUDYING THE TEXT OF 2 CORINTHIANS

Scanning
Paul was having a hard time getting the Corinthians to follow his advice. One reason was that many of the people wouldn't accept his apostleship. So this follow-up letter was intensely personal, showing Paul's feelings. For him the Christian life means being all out for Christ or it isn't real life at all.

We can get a "feel" for this letter by looking quickly over its thirteen chapters, reading the title headings and the opening verses of each paragraph. After that we may want to read the whole book rather quickly. While we read, we could imagine ourselves in Paul's place or as one of the Corinthian believers.

Beginning and End
When we compare the beginning and end of the letter, we see a thankful apostle (1:1-11) and a gracious friend (13:5-14). This inspires us to read on, to learn how an active person can handle heavy burdens.

Overview
There are three main parts in 2 Corinthians. Read the Bible text of these three parts, referring to the following outline and notes along the way:

2 CORINTHIANS: PAUL'S MINISTRY AND GOD'S GIFTS

SALUTATION 1:1,2	SKETCH OF PAUL'S MINISTRY	APPEAL FOR GIVING	DEFENSE OF PAUL'S MINISTRY		CONCLUSION 13:11-14
	1:3	8:1	10:1	13:10	

1. *Sketch of Paul's Ministry* (1:3-7:16)

Good Relations With Fellow Christians (1:3-2:13). After the opening greeting (1:1,2), Paul cleared up false reports about his changed plans to visit Corinth. He wanted the people to know how much he loved them (2:4).

Ministry of the Gospel (2:14-7:3). Paul's subjects here are the

Gospel message itself, his keeping on with preaching even though he was often weary, and his joy in being sent to speak for Christ (5:20).

Joy in Sorrow (7:4-16) "I am greatly encouraged; in all our troubles my joy knows no bounds" (7:4).

2. *Appeal for Giving* (8:1-9:15).

We can learn much from Paul about giving to the Lord's work.

The last verse in this sermon is his high point: "Thanks be to God for his indescribable gift!" (9:15).

3. *Defense of Paul's Ministry* (10:1-13:10)

"Since you are demanding proof that Christ is speaking through me" (13:3). Paul told them why he was God's messenger, including: "The things that mark an apostle—signs, wonders and miracles—were done among you with great perseverance" (12:12). "The authority the Lord gave me for building you up" (13:10). This was Paul's last word about his credentials as an apostle before saying "good-bye" (13:11-14).

Paul's defense was aimed at false apostles and the Corinthian believers whom they led away from Paul's good teaching. We can understand why Paul needed to defend his apostleship. He was taking a stand before the entire Christian world of the first century. Who are the gospel's true ministers, and who are the false? Paul's second Corinthian letter gives the answer for all time to people everywhere.

If studying the New Testament in topical order,
go now to Mark.

GALATIANS

Set Free From Bondage

Setting

The book of Galatians, earliest of thirteen New Testament letters that Paul wrote, is easier to understand when we learn why it was written. On his first missionary journey (Acts 13:1-14:28), Paul with his helpers preached the gospel in cities of south Galatia—Antioch, Iconium, Lystra and Derbe (see map). Many were saved and began worshiping together.

Soon after leaving the area, Paul learned that other teachers had come in and had told the new Christians that Paul was a false teacher who had not preached the *whole* gospel message (Galatians 1:6,7). These troublemakers argued that salvation is by faith in Christ, *and* by taking part in Jewish ceremonies (for example, Jewish circumcision). In other words, they told the Gentile converts of Galatia they were not saved if they did not *also* become practicing Jews.

Paul wrote to the Galatians to repeat the message he had first preached to them, that salvation is through faith alone, *not faith plus something*—such as keeping the Jewish religious laws. "It is for freedom that Christ has set us free. Stand firm, then, and do not let yourselves be burdened again by a yoke of slavery. Mark my words! I, Paul, tell you that if you let yourselves be circumcised, Christ will be of no value to you at all. Again I declare to every man who lets himself be circumcised that he is obligated to obey the whole law. You who are trying to be justified by law have been alienated from Christ; you have fallen away from grace." (5:1-4).

Author
Paul was the writer, and some of his Christian friends joined in sending greetings (1:1,2).

First Readers
Paul wrote to "the churches in Galatia" (1:2).

Date Written
A.D. 48 (before the Jerusalem meeting of A.D. 49—Acts 15).

Purposes
Some of Paul's reasons for writing were: to expose false teachings; to defend his apostleship, which had been challenged; to make clear that salvation is through faith plus nothing; to encourage the Galatian Christians to live in the freedom brought by Christ (5:1), and to bring forth in their lives the fruit of the Spirit (5:22,23).

Theme
Only faith can save us from slavery to the law. We live by following God's Spirit in the freedom Christ has given us.

Key Words
Gospel, law, faith, Spirit, free.

Outline
Set Free in Christ
Introduction 1:1-5
   A. Source of the gospel 1:6-2:21
   B. Defense of the gospel 3:1-5:1

C. Application of the gospel 5:2-6:10
Conclusion 6:11-18

Key Verse
"After beginning with the Spirit, are you now trying to attain your goal by human effort?" (3:3).

STUDYING THE TEXT OF GALATIANS

When we read Galatians we are surprised by Paul's strong feelings. Paul's words were very strong because he had been attacked by liars, and the young Christians he had led to the Lord were being drawn away from their faith in Christ alone by false teachers.

First Reading
The best thing to do is to read the whole letter in one sitting. Keep this short outline in mind:

SALUTATION 1:1-5	PERSONAL TESTIMONY	TEACHING THE TRUTH	LIVING THE TRUTH	CONCLUSION 6:11-18
	GOOD NEWS	LAW	SPIRIT	
	The Good News I Preach Is From God	The Good News Is Better Than the Law	God's Spirit Gives Freedom	
	1:6	3:1	5:2	

Beginning and End
(1:1-5;6:11-18). Usually the beginning and end of a letter are completely personal, but here Paul included parts of his argument: "Paul, an apostle—sent not from men nor by man, but by Jesus Christ" (1:1); "Those who want to make a good impression outwardly are trying to compel you to be circumcised" (6:12).

Repeated Words
Repeated words in each of the three main sections are clues to their themes. For example, we count the word "gospel" fifteen

times in the first section, "law" twenty-nine times in the second section, and "Spirit" ten times in the last section.

Overview
Before we read the letter more slowly, we should have a clear picture of the whole. While reading this letter observe key phrases and lines. Examples are shown here:

The Gospel (1:6-2:21)—personal testimony
"I did not receive [the gospel] from any man" (1:12).
"I received it by revelation from Jesus Christ" (1:12).

The Law (3:1-5:1)—teaching the truth
"Clearly no one is justified before God by the law" (3:11).
"What, then, was the purpose of the law? It was added because of transgressions"(3:19).
"So the law was put in charge to lead us to Christ that we might be justified by faith" (3:24).

The Spirit (5:2-6:10)—living the truth
"Live by the Spirit . . . If you are led by the Spirit, you are not under law" (5:16,18).

If studying the New Testament in topical order,
go now to Ephesians.

EPHESIANS

Christ and the Church

Setting

When we want to think carefully about the wonderful truths of who Christ is and what he did, Ephesians is the book to read. It has been called Paul's masterpiece, the "Grand Canyon" of Scripture. Paul had a great desire to share with his young Christian friends at Ephesus the excitement and joy he had found in Christ. How did this friendship begin?

Paul's first contact with the Ephesians was a very brief visit to their Jewish synagogue, on his second missionary journey in A.D. 52 (Acts 18:19-21). On his third journey (A.D. 52-56) he taught the people of the area for three years (Acts 18:23-21:16). Then, soon after returning to Jerusalem, the apostle was arrested and falsely accused as a troublemaker (Acts 24:5). He was sent to Rome for trial, and it is from there that he wrote Ephesians.

Author

Paul is named twice—in 1:1 and 3:1.

First Readers
The letter was written first to the church at Ephesus, but Paul also wanted the letter to be read by other churches of the region. The local churches were made up of Jews and Gentiles who became believers during Paul's earlier visits.

Date Written
Around A.D. 61-62.

Purpose
Paul had two main reasons for writing, expressed by two prayers (paraphrased):
"I pray that you may know your resources in Christ" (chapters 1-3).
"I pray that you may live consistent with your faith in Christ" (chapters 4-6).

Theme
Christians' lives show their faith in Christ, because of their never ending resources in Christ and the powerful work of God.

Key Words
Church, in Christ, power, riches.

Outline
Christ and the Church
Introduction 1:1,2
    A. Our heritage in Christ 1:3-3:21
        1. Spiritual blessings in Christ 1:3-14
        2. Prayer for spiritual wisdom 1:15-23
        3. Once dead, now alive 2:1-22
        4. Paul's testimony and prayer 3:1-21
    B. Our life in Christ 4:1-6:20
        1. Keeping church unity 4:1-16
        2. Daily walk of Christians 4:17-5:20
        3. Christian behavior in the home 5:21-6:9
        4. The Christian's armor 6:10-20
Conclusion 6:21-24

Key Verses
"[God seated Christ] at his right hand in the heavenly realms, far above all rule and authority, power and dominion, and every

title that can be given, not only in the present age but also in the one to come. And God placed all things under his feet and appointed him to be head over everything for the church" (Ephesians 1:21b,22).

STUDYING THE TEXT OF EPHESIANS

Scanning
In scanning we do several things to give us the feel of the book: turning the pages, reading the segment titles, reading the first verses of the chapters, and reading the introduction (1:1,2) and conclusion (6:21-24) of the letter.

Structure
In looking for the letter's structure, or how it is put together, we pick up a clue at the end of chapter 3: the last word is "Amen," and the last verse (3:21) is a doxology, or praise to God. The word "Amen" divides the book into two parts: the *work* of God (1:3-3:14) and the *walk* of the Christian (4:1-6:20).

Overview
The chart below shows the structure of the letter in other ways. For example: 1) The work of God is always the foundation of the Christian's daily life. 2) Our place in Christ is the secret to the work of Christ in us.

SALUTATION 1:1,2	WORK OF GOD			WALK OF THE CHRISTIAN		CONCLUSION 6:21-24
	1:3	2:1	3:1	4:1	6:10	
	Blessings "in Christ"	Experience of Salvation	Growing in Knowledge and Strength	Christian Behavior	Christian Armor	
	WE IN CHRIST			CHRIST IN US		

Reading Segment by Segment
Read the segments below and observe key phrases and lines. Now read the main sections of Ephesians, picturing how each part fits into the whole book.

Blessings in Christ (1:3-23). See how often the words "in Christ" appear in 1:3-14. This is an important section in this letter, and has the title, "Spiritual Blessings in Christ." The prayers of 1:15-23 and 3:14-21 are among the greatest in Scripture.

Experience of Salvation (2:1-22) "For it is by grace you have been saved, through faith—and this not from yourselves, it is the gift of God" (2:8, see also 2:5).

Growing in Knowledge and Strength (3:1-20). "And I pray that you . . . may have power, together with all the saints, to grasp how wide and long and high and deep is the love of Christ" (3:18). "I pray that out of his glorious riches he may strengthen you with power through his Spirit"(3:16).

Christian Behavior (4:1-6:9). "You must no longer live as the Gentiles do, in the futility of their thinking" (4:17).

Christian Armor (6:10-20). "Put on the full armor of God so that you can take your stand against the devil's schemes" (6:11). Revelation 2:1-6 describes the Ephesian church's spiritual condition thirty-five years later.

If studying the New Testament in topical order, go now to Philippians.

PHILIPPIANS

Life in Christ

Setting

Philippi is often called the birthplace of European Christianity, because the book of Acts records that the first believer in Europe was saved here (Acts 16:14,15). This happened around A.D. 50, on Paul's second missionary journey (Acts 16:12-40). Paul gained many new friends in Philippi during his missionary journey, and they continued to be a source of joy in the years that followed (1:3-8). Paul also suffered persecution in Philippi (1 Thessalonians 2:2).

After Paul's first visit at Philippi, his friend Luke remained behind to teach the new believers and help them start a church. By the time Paul writes them a letter from Rome, six years later, the church was a growing fellowship (1:1).

Philippians is the most joyful of all Paul's writings. There is less correction and more praise in Philippians than in any other New Testament letter. Down through the ages Philippians has helped renew the spiritual life of many Christians.

Author
Paul was the writer, and Timothy was his helper (1:1).

First Readers
Paul sent the letter to "all the saints in Christ Jesus at Philippi," and their "overseers and deacons" (1:1).

Place and Date of Writing
Paul wrote Philippians from his rented house in Rome, where he was imprisoned around A.D. 61-62. Luke tells about these two years under prison guards in Acts 28:16-31.

Purposes
Paul had many practical reasons for writing. He taught important beliefs (2:6-11), but he always attached commands and advice to them (2:5). Most of the teachings are about a life centered in Christ (1:20,21; 3:7-14). And throughout the letter Paul overflowed with thanksgiving for the friendship he enjoyed with the people. The letter has been called Paul's love letter to the believers at Philippi.

Theme
The secret of true joy for the believer is living in Christ.

Key Words
Joy, in Christ, Spirit, love.

Outline
   Life in Christ
   Introduction 1:1-2
      A. Christ Our Life 1:3-26
      B. Christ Our Example 1:27-2:30
      C. Christ Our Goal 3:1-4:1
      D. Christ Our Supply 4:2-20
   Greetings and Blessing 4:21-23

Key Verse
"For to me, to live is Christ and to die is gain" (1:21).

STUDYING THE TEXT OF PHILIPPIANS

First Readings
The letter is short, so it's easy to read in one sitting. This is the time for first thoughts and feelings.

Key Word
Joy. A good exercise is to scan the letter again and mark every appearance of the word joy and words such as happy and rejoice.

Overview
It's hard to find any outline in Philippians. This may be partly because the letter is very personal and informal.

TESTIMONY	EXAMPLES		TEACHING
Present Attitudes ➡	Aims and Desires	⬅	Present Sufficiency
CHRIST OUR LIFE	CHRIST OUR EXAMPLE	CHRIST OUR GOAL	CHRIST OUR SUPPLY
1:1	1:27	3:1	4:2

Further Readings
Now is a good time to read the segments of the Bible text. As we read, keep in mind the theme, *Life in Christ*, suggested by the key verse, "For to me, to live is Christ" (1:21). We'll follow our outline on the chart as we read the text, and look for key phrases.

Christ Our Life (1:1-26). The reason Paul prays for his friends, loves them dearly, and handles troubles without giving up the Lord's work is Christ.

Christ Our Example (1:27-2:30). A great Bible passage is 2:5-11, about Christ being a humble servant and yet being raised to highest honor by God. It is one of the most wonderful passages in the Bible. We should try to memorize it.

Christ Our Goal (3:1-4:1). Chapter 3 is the mountain peak of Philippians. "I want to know Christ and the power of his resurrection and the fellowship of sharing in his sufferings, becoming like him in his death" (3:10). "I press on toward the goal to win the prize for which God has called me heavenward in Christ Jesus" (3:14).

Christ Our Supply (4:2-23). Christ supplies or meets all our needs. One of Paul's last commands is about joy: "Rejoice in the Lord always" (4:4). The verses 4:4-7 are powerful and uplifting advice for all believers.

There can be no real joy outside of Jesus Christ. He is the Christian's life (1:21), best example (2:5-11), great goal (3:10), and generous provider (4:13).

If studying the New Testament in topical order, go now to Colossians

Three Letters Compared

We can't help but notice how different Paul's letters are from each other, as shown by this chart:

GALATIANS, EPHESIANS and PHILIPPIANS COMPARED

	GALATIANS	EPHESIANS	PHILIPPIANS
Style	mainly logic and argument	doctrine and exhortation	information and consolation
A Main Subject	Salvation	Christ the Savior	Life of Joy
Purpose	correction	edification	inspiration
Tone	sharp, rebuking	calm, victorious	tender, joyful

COLOSSIANS

Christ *Is* All and *In* All

Setting

False religious groups called cults have always been around, twisting and denying the truth and tempting people away from the true word of God. Colossians is a good book to read, because it shows how Paul handled the false teachings of the cults in the church at Colosse.

All of Paul's letters from prison, including Colossians, give much attention to Jesus Christ. The differences in the letters are in purposes or aims. For example, in Ephesians Paul focused on *Christ and the Church*, while in Colossians he wrote about *Christ and the Universe*, "things in heaven and on earth" (1:16).

Author

The opening words say this letter is "from Paul." His helper Timothy sent greetings also (1:1).

First Readers
Paul sent the letter to the church at Colosse (1:2), and he asked them to share the letter with the church in nearby Laodicea (4:16). Colosse is a small town 100 miles inland from Ephesus. Paul's three-year evangelistic and teaching work around Ephesus on his third missionary journey probably had much to do with the founding of the church at Colosse. Epaphras (1:7) and Archippus (4:17) were leaders of the congregation.

Date Written
Paul wrote from his prison quarters in Rome, around A.D. 61.

Purpose
Paul wrote especially to challenge and expose the heresies or false beliefs that were being taught in the churches at Colosse and neighboring areas. Among the heresies were these: 1) Jewish religious requirements such as circumcision (2:11; 3:11), rules to follow (2:14), foods and religious holidays (2:16); 2) a severe self-denial (2:16,20-23); 3) worship of angels (2:18); and 4) too high an opinion, almost a worship, of knowledge (2:8). Paul exploded the heresies by presenting the truth about who Jesus Christ is and what he did for us.

Theme
Christ is all that is important (3:11).

Key Words
All, pray, knowledge, love.

Outline
  Christ Is *All and* In *All*
  Introduction 1:1-2
    A. Christian thanksgiving 1:3-12
    B. True beliefs 1:13-2:5
    C. False beliefs 2:6-23
    D. Christian living 3:1-4:6
    E. Christian fellowship 4:7-18

Key Verses
"All things were created by him and for him. He is before all things, and in him all things hold together" (Colossians 1:16b,17).

STUDYING THE TEXT OF COLOSSIANS

Scanning
First do the usual scanning of the Bible text to get the feel of the passage and its general purpose.

Overview
Most of the New Testament letters have at least these three kinds of content: personal remarks or concerns, teaching and practical advice. The personal sections, involving people in the churches being written to, usually appear at the beginning and end of the letter. The teaching sections come before the practical, because the writer wanted first to point out God's truth and rules for life and living so that he could apply this truth to the real experiences of the reader.

MAINLY PERSONAL	MAINLY TEACHING		MAINLY PRACTICAL	MAINLY PERSONAL
Christian Thanksgiving	True Beliefs	False Beliefs	Christian Living	Christian Fellowship
CHRIST YOUR INHERITANCE	CHRIST LIVING IN YOU	CHRIST YOUR FOUNDATION	CHRIST YOUR GOAL	CHRIST YOUR MASTER
1:1	1:13	2:6	3:1	4:7

When a letter like Colossians exposes false teaching, it will first teach the true beliefs that are being violated and then expose the false beliefs.

Important Passages
Spend extra time reading about these subjects in the letter:

Thanksgiving and Intercession (1:3-12). "We have not stopped praying for you and asking God to fill you with the knowledge of his will" (1:9).

Person and Work of Christ (1:13-2:5). The phrases around the repeated word "all" in 1:15-20 show much about Jesus, because later in the letters Paul will expose the false teaching in the church. "All things hold together" because of him (1:17). The context (the verses before and after this one) shows that the phrase "all things" refers to both the physical and spiritual realms. About the first, physical scientists often wonder what force keeps the atoms of the universe from flying apart, "holding them together." Paul gave the answer in 1:17. It is Christ, the very one whose power was rejected by the Colossian heresy.

Heresies Exposed (2:6-23). These are the false teachings cited above. We see in the letter that Paul doesn't *name* the heresies.

Christianity in Action (3:1-4:18). The practical and personal sections are filled with plain, clear teaching and commands that show *real* Christian living. Example: "Devote yourselves to prayer, being watchful and thankful" (4:2).

*If studying the New Testament in topical order,
go now to Philemon.*

1 THESSALONIANS

The Lord Jesus Is Coming Again

Setting

Jesus' first coming to earth was an event of great importance. His second coming will be the climax of world history. He came the first time to die and conquer death. When he comes again, it will be to gather to himself those who belong to him, and to rule as their King. Paul summed up all the joy and glories of this coming by saying simply with confidence, "And so we will be with the Lord forever" (4:17). It's no wonder that the gospel is good news.

In the Thessalonian letters Paul focused on the theme of Christ's return. The apostle not only gave the details of final events but he also showed how Christians should live day by day aware of the Lord's return. We can't read and study these letters without growing stronger in our Christian faith and deeds.

Author

Paul wrote the letter (1:1).

First Readers
Paul wrote to new Christians at Thessalonica. He had led them to the Lord only two years earlier, on his second missionary journey (Acts 17:1-10).

Thessalonica was the capital of the province of Macedonia. It was an important trade center of about 200,000 people, mostly Greeks, but also many Jews.

Date Written
Paul wrote the letter around A.D. 52, after he wrote Galatians.

Purposes
Paul had several purposes in writing, including the encouragement of new Christians, urging them to live godly lives, correcting errors in their understanding of the Christian faith, and exposing sins and faults, and showing how Christ's return relates to the life and death of a believer.

Theme
The Lord Jesus is coming again.

Key Words
Brothers, coming, word, day, love.

Outline
Jesus Is Coming Again
Greeting 1:1
Looking Back 1:2-3:13
   A. Conversion and testimony 1:2-2:16
   B. Paul's service 2:17-3:13
Looking Forward 4:1-5:24
   A. Daily walk 4:1-12
   B. Lord's return 4:13-5:24
Conclusion 5:25-28

Key Verses
"May your whole spirit, soul and body be kept blameless at the coming of our Lord Jesus Christ. The one who calls you is faithful and he will do it" (5:23,24).

STUDYING THE TEXT OF 1 THESSALONIANS

Scanning
We can read 1 Thessalonians easily in one sitting. Get a feel of
the letter and observe its highlights. Note the short greeting (1:1)
and conclusion (5:25-28). It is interesting to observe that each
chapter ends with a word about the Lord's return.

"to wait for his Son from heaven"	1:10
"the crown in which we will glory in the presence of our Lord Jesus when he comes"	2:19
"when our Lord Jesus comes with all his holy ones"	3:13
we will "meet the Lord in the air"	4:17
"be kept blameless at the coming of our Lord Jesus Christ"	5:23

This would be a good time to read the entire letter again and
notice what Paul said in each chapter leading up to those final
words about Jesus' second coming.

Overview
The following chart can give us some direction as we read the
letter:

SALUTATION 1:1	LOOKING BACK			LOOKING FORWARD		CONCLUSION 5:25-28
	Thessalonians' Turning to Christ	Paul's Service		Daily Walk	Final Day of the Lord Will Come	
	1:2	2:1	3:1	4:1	4:13	

The arrangement of the text is shown in two ways: backward
and forward. Note key phrases in each:

Looking Back (1:2-3:13).
"You became a model to all the believers" (1:7)
"We were gentle among you" (2:7)
"We sent Timothy . . . to strengthen and encourage you" (3:2)

Looking Forward (4:1-5:24). Paul indicates a change of direction: "Finally, brothers" (4:1). He wanted his readers to look into the future: "Now we ask you and urge you in the Lord Jesus to do this more and more" (4:1). "The Lord himself will come down from heaven" (4:16). And when he does, those Christians living and those who have already died will be "caught up . . . in the clouds to meet the Lord in the air" (4:17). This passage is the highlight of the letter. "The dead in Christ will rise first" (4:16). "This day should [not] surprise you like a thief" (5:4).

*If studying the New Testament in topical order,
go now to 2 Thessalonians.*

2 THESSALONIANS

The Day of the Lord Has Not Come Yet

Setting

After Paul wrote 1 Thessalonians, some of the people in the church got the wrong idea about his teaching on the coming "day of the Lord" in the clouds to "take up" (rapture) the saints, dead and living, to heaven (1 Thessalonians 4:13-18). The Thessalonians then spread the word that the day had already come (2 Thessalonians 2:2) and that was why they were experiencing persecution (2 Thessalonians 1:4). Paul wanted to correct that wrong belief by saying that the time of eternal punishment was yet to come (1:7-10).

Author

The name Paul appears in 1:1 and 3:17.

First Readers

Paul wrote to the same people addressed in the first letter, the new Christians at Thessalonica.

Date Written
A.D. 52, a few months after the first letter.

Purposes
The letter praises the Thessalonian Christians for their growing faith in the midst of persecution, assures them of his prayer
support, and corrects the false understanding of Paul's teaching
about the "day of the Lord" in his first letter to them.

Theme
The Day of the Lord will not come until after the man of evil
has appeared.

Key Words
Lord, evil, Day, punish, pray, work, glory.

Outline
  The Day of the Lord Has Not Come Yet
  Greeting 1:1,2
    A. Don't be disturbed 1:3-12
    B. Stand firm 2:1-17
    C. Work 3:1-15
  Conclusion 3:16-18

Key Verses
*"The coming of the lawless one will be in accordance with the
work of Satan displayed in all kinds of counterfeit miracles, signs
and wonders, and in every sort of evil that deceives those who are
perishing. They perish because they refused to love the truth and
so be saved" (2 Thessalonians 2:9,10).*

STUDYING THE TEXT OF 2 THESSALONIANS

Scanning
The entire letter has just forty-seven verses, but it is interesting
to see that eighteen of these are about end times. This is a strong
clue to the letter's main purpose.

Beginning and End
The greeting is brief (1:1,2), and the sign-off a little longer
(3:16-18).

The Main Point

The whole letter turns around Paul's answer to the Thessalonians' wrong understanding. Paul argued that the "day of the Lord" had *not* already come. Because of that, he wrote, Christians should not be disturbed or confused over their suffering (1:3-10). They should stand strong and continue to believe the teachings he gave them (2:13-17), and productive work should be their daily habit (3:6-15).

Overview

When we read the Bible text we will get help by referring to this survey chart:

2 THESSALONIANS: THE DAY OF THE LORD HAS NOT COME YET

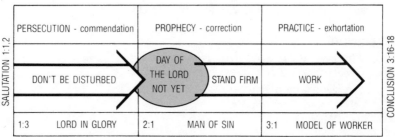

As we read the Bible text slowly we should observe key phrases and lines about the subjects below:

Lord in Glory (1:3-12). Paul showed how Christians are involved in Christ's glory. We look to see how persecutions are related to that glory (1:4-10). "God is just: He will pay back trouble to those who trouble you and give relief to you who are troubled" (1:6,7).

Man of Evil (2:1-17). This is the antichrist of the end times. Paul wrote that the day of the Lord will not come until two things have happened: first, a great rebellion against God (2:3). And then the man of evil will appear, the one who will encourage rebellion against God. Chapter 2 is the key chapter of this letter, and we should spend much time here. What about this antichrist? Paul wrote: "He will oppose and will exalt himself over everything that is called God or is worshiped" (2:4). "Proclaiming himself to be God" (2:4). "And then the lawless one will be revealed, whom the Lord Jesus will overthrow with the breath of his mouth and destroy by the splendor of his coming" (2:8).

Work Until He Comes (3:6-15). Much is written in this letter about the importance of work as it relates to persecution, antichrist and the "day of the Lord." One may ask, why so much attention to work? We should look for answers because they are there: "We hear that some among you are idle. They are not busy; they are busy-bodies." (3:11). "And as for you, brothers, never tire of doing what is right" (3:13, also see 1:11).

The Lord Jesus is coming again, says 1 Thessalonians. He has not come yet, says 2 Thessalonians. May we, his servants on earth, be faithful until he comes.

If studying the New Testament in topical order,
go now to 1 Peter.

1 TIMOTHY

Pastors and Laymen in Churches

Setting

Living in this world is not easy. Paul called it a "fight." He told his friend Timothy to "fight the good fight" of faith (1 Timothy 1:18). Why did he use such strong words? For our answer, we go back to Paul's third missionary journey, when he and his helper Timothy spent about three years preaching and teaching the gospel in Ephesus and the surrounding area (Acts 18:23-21:17). After he returned to Jerusalem, Paul was sent to prison in Rome (Acts 21:18-28:31). While there, he sent the Ephesian church a letter praising the people for their holy walk with Jesus (Ephesians 1:15,16). But soon Paul began to hear reports of problems that were hurting the churches there.

After Paul was released from prison, he and Timothy visited the churches around Ephesus and saw the problems. Paul asked Timothy to stay at Ephesus and help work out the problems (1 Timothy 1:3). Paul later found out that he would be delayed in returning to Ephesus. So he wrote this first letter to Timothy

(3:14,15). Paul wanted Timothy and all the pastors and church leaders to face their spiritual enemies head-on, in the power of God. We call this letter a pastoral letter. Timothy did not pastor a church himself, but worked as Paul's helper.

Author
Paul, "an apostle of Christ Jesus," wrote to his spiritual son Timothy.

First Readers
The letter was to Timothy, but Timothy was to share the message with all the people: "Point these things out to the brothers" (4:6).

Date Written
A.D. 62, soon after Paul left Timothy at Ephesus.

Purposes
Paul wrote to help Timothy train leaders in the churches and to encourage him and the people to grow in their Christian lives.

Theme
Christians must watch their lives, deeds and teaching with great care.

Key Words
Serve God, teach, command, love, man of God.

Outline
Pastors and People in Churches
Greeting 1:1,2
Command to Timothy 1:3-20
  A. Sound doctrine 1:3-11
  B. Grace and warfare 1:12-20
Instructions to Timothy 2:1-6:21a
  A. Public worship in the church 2:1-15
  B. Church leaders 3:1-13
  C. Hymn of worship 3:14-16
  D. Help to fight false teaching 4:1-16
  E. Widows, elders and slaves 5:1-6:2a
  F. Final instructions 6:2b-21a
Blessing 6:21b

Key Verse
"Timothy, guard what has been entrusted to your care. Turn away from godless chatter and the opposing ideas of what is falsely called knowledge" (6:20).

STUDYING THE TEXT OF 1 TIMOTHY

Scanning
Reading the eleven segment headings of these six chapters will show the highlights of the letter.

Beginning and End
Both parts are short benedictions of good wishes (1:1,2 and the last line of 6:21).

Three Hymns
Paul put three short hymns in the letter. When we read each hymn, we should also read the paragraph leading up to it.

Hymn (1) "Honor and glory forever!" (1:17)
Hymn (2) "Our life of worship" (3:16)
Hymn (3) "God is the blessed and only Ruler" (6:15,16)

The entire letter deals with needs and problems, but the bright tone of victory is there, too. The reason for this is Paul's great faith in such a powerful God and loving Lord. It made him want to sing hymns!

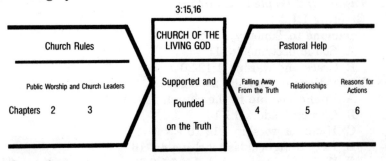

Overview
Paul has two main purposes in his letter to Timothy—a command, and some instructions.

Command to Timothy (1:3-20). The command concerns Timothy's big task. In the middle of the command, Paul gives his testimony (1:12-17). "I thank Christ Jesus our Lord because he trusted me and gave me this work of serving him" (see 1:12). In the surrounding paragraphs (verses 3-11 and verses 18-20) Paul gave orders to Timothy, such as: "Command them to stop" teaching false things (1:3). "Holding on to faith and a good conscience" (1:19).

Instructions to Timothy (2:1-6:21). The central point of these five chapters is the hymn of 3:15,16, shown on the chart above. Whether Paul was giving Timothy instructions for the church or pastoral help, he realized this is the "church of the living God, the pillar and foundation of the truth" (3:15).

It is important to see that the message of the gospel as stated in the six lines of 3:16 is a key part of worship. Read these lines carefully.

If studying the New Testament in topical order,
go now to Titus.

2 TIMOTHY

Endurance and Separation

Setting

This is the last letter Paul wrote. It is tender and loving. Paul was old when he wrote 2 Timothy. He was in a cold, dark, Roman jail. He knew he had only a short time left to live (4:6). So the letter is his spiritual last will and testament—his "dying wish"— to his friend and co-worker Timothy.

It has been five years since Paul wrote 1 Timothy. Christians throughout the Roman Empire were suffering for their faith. Cruel Emperor Nero was trying to wipe out Christianity. That's why Paul was back in prison. The first time Paul went to prison in Rome (A.D. 58-62), he expected to be set free (Philippians 1:24-26). This time he expected to be killed (2 Timothy 4:6).

Author

The letter is from "Paul, an apostle of Christ Jesus by the will of God" (1:1).

First Readers
The whole letter was Paul's farewell to his friend Timothy. He included messages that he wanted Timothy to deliver to friends. The last short blessing, "Grace be with you [plural]" (4:22) was to everyone Paul knew.

Date Written
A.D. 67.

Purposes
Paul wrote out of a lonely heart, saying a warm "good-bye" to his dear friend. His main spiritual purpose was to inspire and challenge Timothy to go on with the gospel ministry.

Theme
Christian workers approved by the Lord endure problems, avoid evil people, make known the good news and teach the Word of God.

Key Words
Suffer troubles, not ashamed, command, Word, endure, worker.

Outline
Endurance and Separation
Salutation 1:1-2
    A. Challenge to share in suffering 1:3-2:13
    B. Challenge to separate from evil people 2:14-4:5
    C. Parting words 4:6-8
    D. Personal instructions 4:9-18
Greetings and benediction 4:19-22

Key Verses
"The Lord stood at my side and gave me strength, so that through me the message might be fully proclaimed and all the Gentiles might hear it. And I was delivered from the lion's mouth. The Lord will rescue me from every evil attack and will bring me safely to his heavenly kingdom. To him be glory for ever and ever. Amen" (2 Timothy 4:17,18).

STUDYING THE TEXT OF 2 TIMOTHY

First Readings
This is the kind of letter we want to read many times because it speaks to our hearts and makes us want to listen carefully to the "dying words" of a great man of God.

Tone
After reading the letter we can understand why it has been called "a letter mixed with gloom and glory." There is tenderness and sadness in such lines as these: "Recalling your tears" (1:4); "do not be ashamed . . . of me" (1:8); "everyone deserted me" (4:16); "the time has come for my departure" (4:6). But the main tone of the letter, even when talking about suffering, is triumph, and glory, and deep thankfulness: "By the power of God" (1:8); "You, however, know all about my teaching, my way of life, my purpose, faith, patience, love, endurance" (3:10); "there is in store for me the crown of righteousness" (4:8); "to him be glory forever and ever" (4:18).

Beginning and End
The greeting is brief (1:1,2). But the end of the letter is long. There are personal words, instructions and testimonies (4:9-18), followed by greetings and a benediction (4:19-22).

Overview
The main part of the letter, leading to a climax in 4:6-8, gives two challenges.

2 TIMOTHY: ENDURANCE AND SEPARATION

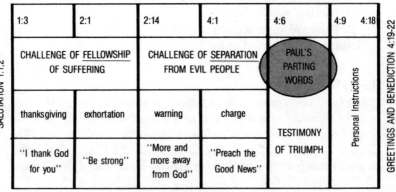

Challenge to Share in Suffering (1:3—2:13). The key messages are, "Join with me in suffering" (1:8) and "Endure hardship with us like a good soldier of Christ Jesus" (2:3). Paul could patiently accept all the troubles caused by witnessing for Christ, knowing that many would be saved (2:10). So now he challenges Timothy to suffer *with him* "for the gospel" (1:8).

Challenge to Separate From Evil People (2:14—4:5). The key message is, "Have nothing to do with them" (3:5). The whole paragraph where this verse appears shows the many different sins of these evil people (3:1-9). Paul told Timothy to follow the right ways of the Holy Scriptures as he had learned through his parents and teachers. Paul gave Timothy instructions: "Preach the Word; be prepared in season and out of season . . . do the work of an evangelist, discharge all the duties of your ministry" (4:2,5).

We see that the letter leads to a climax, which is the final, moving testimony of Paul (4:6-8). He had finished the race, and now a crown was waiting for him (4:7,8).

Important Passages
These are key passages of 2 Timothy:

Last days	3:1-9,13
God-inspired Scriptures	3:16,17
Paul's farewell	4:1-22

If studying the New Testament in topical order, go now to John.

TITUS

Doing God's Work

Setting

No one can be saved by good works, but good works have an important place in the Christian's life. Titus has much to say about this.

Soon after Paul wrote 1 Timothy to his closest friend, he and another co-worker, Titus, did evangelistic work in the towns of Crete, an island south of Greece. Paul left Titus there to finish the work (1:5), and from Nicopolis Paul wrote him the letter we now call Titus (3:12). The letter is addressed to Titus, but Paul intended that Titus share the message with the Cretan people ("You must teach" 2:1; "Remind the people" 3:1).

The men Timothy and Titus were alike in many ways—both were young, gifted co-workers of Paul, probably converted through the apostle's ministry. Both men served as Paul's representatives in difficult churches.

The Cretan people had a bad reputation in the Mediterranean world: "Cretans are always liars, evil brutes, lazy gluttons" (1:12). Some of these islanders had become Christians, and Paul wanted to encourage them to live like Christians. "For the grace of God that brings salvation has appeared to all men. It teaches us to say 'No' to ungodliness and worldly passions, and to live self-controlled, upright and godly lives in this present age" (2:11,12). Over and over again in the letter Paul wrote about *doing good deeds*.

Author
Paul wrote the letter while traveling to Nicopolis, in northern Macedonia.

First Readers
The letter is addressed to Titus (1:4), but Paul wanted Titus to share the message with all the Cretans.

Date Written
A.D. 62, soon after writing 1 Timothy.

Purposes
The purposes were: to remind Titus that his task is to supervise the churches and to encourage the Christians about *doing good deeds* in everyday living.

Theme
Jesus Christ died to free us from all evil, to make us people who are "eager to do what is good" (2:14).

Key Words
Good deeds, do good, teach, true teaching, grace.

Outline
  Doing Good Deeds
  Introduction 1:1-4
    A. Leaders of an orderly church 1:5-16
    B. Laity of a sound church 2:1-15
    C. Members of a practicing church 3:1-11
  Conclusion 3:12-15

Key Verses
"We lived in malice and envy, being hated and hating one another. But when the kindness and love of God our Savior appeared, he saved us, not because of righteous things we had done, but because of his mercy" (Titus 3:3-5).

STUDYING THE TEXT OF TITUS

Scanning
The letter is short, and Paul's instructions to Titus are to the point. We should have pencil in hand as we read the letter, marking words and phrases that stand out.

Beginning and End
The greeting is simple—"From Paul" (1:1) . . . "To Titus" (1:4)— but between those phrases is a beautiful statement about preaching God's truth to the world.

The conclusion (3:12-15) has the usual personal notes, and we see that Paul repeated the theme of his letter: "Our people must learn to use their lives for *doing good deeds*. They should do good to those in need. Then our people will not have useless lives" (3:14). Useless lives! Who wants a useless life?

Two Great Statements
The two paragraphs 2:11-14 and 3:4-7 are two of the most complete statements of Christian truth in the New Testament. We should read them carefully. Later we can see how Paul used them to support his theme.

Repeated Words
Paul used certain words over and over again. Some of these are: *doing good deeds* and *teaching*.

Overview
Paul's topics in this letter were: 1) a church must be built on order and truth; 2) good leadership is a key to good followers; 3) good deeds should be the life-style of everyone in the church, both leaders and lay people.

INTRODUCTION 1:1-4	LEADERS 1:5	LAITY 2:1	- old - young - slaves - masters	GENERAL 3:1	CONCLUSION 3:12-15
	Orderly Church	Sound Church Built on Truth		Practicing Church	
	leaders	opponents (10)	followers		

Important Passages
Read more than once these important passages of Titus:

False Teaching in a Church (1:1-16). False teaching is best dealt with by true teaching (1:1-4).

Making the Gospel Attractive (2:1-10). Paul tells how our deeds can show others that God's teaching is good.

The Grace of God (2:11-14; 3:4-7). "For the grace of God that brings salvation has appeared to all men. It teaches us to say 'No' to ungodliness and worldly passions, and to live self-controlled, upright, and godly lives in this present age" (2:11,12).

If studying the New Testament in topical order,
go now to 2 Timothy.

PHILEMON

Appeal for Forgiveness

Setting

A forgiving spirit is so important that Jesus included forgiveness in the prayer he taught his disciples (Matthew 6:12). Paul believed that forgiveness was a way of showing Christian love. This forgiveness was the reason he wrote to his friend Philemon. Picture the setting that caused Paul to write this letter.

Philemon was a well-to-do Christian friend of Paul, living in or near Colosse. He was probably a member of the small Colossian church. It appears that one of Philemon's slaves, Onesimus, had stolen something from his master. Fearing punishment he fled to Rome like so many other runaway slaves.

In Rome, Onesimus came to know Paul, who was in his Roman prison quarters (Acts 28:16,30,31). Paul had the joy of helping Onesimus give his life to the Lord Jesus Christ (Philemon 10). Now Paul was concerned that Onesimus get back together with Philemon. But he didn't want Onesimus to be punished. So he wrote this tender and heart-moving letter to ask Philemon to forgive and free Onesimus. The letter was carried to Philemon by Onesimus and Tychicus, who also delivered the letters known as Ephesians and Colossians to the churches in those cities (Colossians 4:7-9).

Author
Paul wrote the letter and Timothy joined him in sending greetings (verse 1).

First Readers
The letter was for Philemon, but Paul also sent greetings to Philemon's wife, Apphia, and their son, Archippus, and to the church that met in their home (verse 2).

Date Written
Around A.D. 61.

Purpose
Paul asked Philemon to forgive Onesimus and accept him back as a brother in Christ (16).

Theme
The whole letter is one Christian's plea to another Christian to forgive and restore a third Christian.

Key Words
Love, slave, favor, welcome. Note: the word "forgive" does not appear in the letter, but the spirit of forgiveness is clear in such phrases as, "welcome him" (17).

Outline
  Appeal for Forgiveness
  Greeting 1:3
    A. Object of the appeal 4-7
    B. The appeal 8-16
    C. Source of the appeal 17-21
  Conclusion and blessing 22-25

Key Verse
"If he has done you any wrong or owes you anything, charge it to me" (Philemon 18).

STUDYING THE TEXT OF PHILEMON

Scanning
The letter is short, like the average letter written by people to-day. Probably that is why it is placed last in the list of Paul's writings.

Beginning and End
Paul began and closed his letter in his usual style: the introduction is a greeting and blessing (1-3); the conclusion has personal notes, greetings, and another blessing (22-25).

Style
The letter is a masterpiece of graceful, careful, and polite asking for a forgiving spirit. This very personal letter of Paul has been called a "model letter written by a master of letter writing."

Overview
When we read this letter, we may be suprised at how *organized* a friendly, personal message can be. Follow the outline, as you read the Bible text.

PHILEMON: APPEAL FOR FORGIVENESS

SALUTATION 1-3	OBJECT OF THE APPEAL: Philemon's love	THE APPEAL: for a new relationship	SOURCE OF THE APPEAL: Paul's love	CONCLUSION 22-25
	praise of Philemon	plea for Onesimus	promise of Paul	
	4	8	17 21	

Object of the Appeal (4-7). Paul asked for Philemon's help because of his Christian love and faith. "I hear about the love you have for all God's holy people and the faith you have in the Lord Jesus" (5). "You, brother, have refreshed the hearts of the saints" (7).

The Appeal (8-16). Paul told Philemon that Onesimus was a changed man now that he was a believer. He "became my son" (10), who "has become useful both to you and to me" (11). (This is a play on words because Onesimus means "useful.") Paul tells Philemon why he would want to have Onesimus back. "He is very dear to me but even dearer to you, both as a man and as a brother in the Lord" (16).

Source of the Appeal (17-21). Paul reminded Philemon of their friendship. "If you consider me a partner, welcome him" (17). I know that "you will do even more than I ask" (21).

Re-reading
Go back now and re-read the letter, looking for all that can be learned about forgiveness, including the role that God the Father, the Son and the Spirit have in this.

Illustration of Christ's Work for the Sinner
Paul pleads for this slave, as Christ pleads for us sinners, before his Father in heaven:
"welcome him as you would welcome me" (17)
"charge it to me" (18)
"I will pay it back" (19)

Slavery in New Testament Times
In this letter to Philemon, Paul doesn't attack slavery. Rather, he gives principles of Christian behavior and relationships between brothers in Christ that will bring about the end of slavery.

If studying the New Testament in topical order,
go now to 1 Timothy.

HEBREWS

Consider Jesus, Our Great High Priest

Setting

The book of Hebrews shows how Christ fulfills the teaching of the Old Testament. All the ceremonies, such as the priests' offerings of sacrifices, were examples pointing forward to Christ, who is the great Sacrifice for sin.

Hebrews was written because of a spiritual need. The Jewish Christians addressed by the letter were losing sight of God's Son, their all-sufficient Savior, and were turning more and more to their old life-style. "Fix your thoughts on Jesus!" (3:1) is the book's urgent call to believers.

This exciting book has been called the "fifth Gospel" because it tells of Jesus' work on earth ("he died for everyone," see 2:9) and his work in heaven ("we have a great high priest" 4:14). Just as God led the Israelites from Egypt to Canaan through all kinds of dangers and troubles, so Christ today is helping his children enter into the spiritual rest-land of a full life, giving a taste of the heavenly glories to come.

Author
The author of Hebrews is unknown. Paul, Barnabas, Apollos and another co-worker of Paul have been suggested as possible writers.

First Readers
The letter was sent to a congregation of Jewish Christians living somewhere in the Roman world such as Jerusalem, Rome, or Ephesus. The many strong warnings in the book indicate that the readers were in a poor spiritual condition, turning from Christ to their former Jewish beliefs.

Date Written
Between A.D. 65 and 69 (before the destruction of Jerusalem in A.D. 70).

Purpose
The purpose of the letter to the Hebrews was to re-light a dying fire through teaching, warning, and encouraging—centered on Jesus Christ. Even the opening lines show this tremendous truth: God "has spoken to us by his Son" (1:2).

Theme
We have a great high Priest who is Jesus!

Key Words
Better, high priest, Son, faith, agreement (covenant), perfect, eternal.

Outline
Jesus, Our Great High Priest
   A. Superior Person Is Jesus Christ 1:1-7:28
   B. Superior Work of Jesus Christ 8:1-10:18
   C. Superior Life in Jesus Christ 10:19-13:25

Key Verse
"Therefore, since we have a great high priest who has gone through the heavens, Jesus the Son of God, let us hold firmly to the faith we profess"(4:14).

STUDYING THE TEXT OF HEBREWS

Scanning
We can get an early "feel" for the book by reading its segment headings as we turn the pages of the thirteen chapters.

Beginning and End
The closing verses (13:17-25) read as if they were written by Paul, with personal notes and blessings. But the opening verses (1:1-3) are *not* in Paul's style, without a greeting. The opening words show the book's theme: "God has spoken"—revelation, "through his Son"—the person Jesus, "[who] sat down"—finished work of Jesus (1:2-3).

Five Warnings
These serious passages warn the readers of punishment for sin:
"we must be more careful" 2:1-4
"let us try hard to enter God's rest" 3:7-4:13
"then they fell away from Christ!" 5:11-6:20
"there is no longer any sacrifice for sins"   10:26-31
"do not refuse to listen when God speaks"   12:25-29

When we read these warnings, we should think about our own lives. In the context of the warning we'll find ways to appropriate God's power, and incentives to press on to fuller stature as Christians.

Overview
The organization of Hebrews is first instruction (1:1-10:18) and then application (10:19-13:25). The order is intentional: the abundant or full life of the Christian is possible only because of the superior person, Jesus Christ, who lives in the believer, and the superior help he gives to live a godly life.

Main Part of the Letter (1:1-7:28)
First, we read in 8:1: "The point of what we are saying is this:". The writer, looking back over chapters 1-7, viewed them as answers to the question, "What does the Christian have?" Then he sums it up in one statement: We have a high priest who sits on the right side of God's throne in heaven (8:1). The middle section, 8:1-10:18, explains the work of this superior or great high priest, Jesus. There is no one like Christ. There is no intercessor

like him. No animal sacrifice that was offered by a Jewish priest can ever compare with the perfect sacrifice of Christ. This is what we have, *"therefore"* (10:19), *"let us* draw near to God" (10:22). The section 10:19-13:25 is filled with teaching about how to live out in our lives what we have in Christ.

HEBREWS: CONSIDER JESUS, OUR GREAT HIGH PRIEST

INSTRUCTION		APPLICATION
SUPERIOR PERSON	SUPERIOR MINISTRIES	ABUNDANT LIFE
"What have we?"	"We have <u>SUCH</u> A HIGH PRIEST"	"Having . . . therefore . . . <u>let us</u>"
1:1	8:1	10:19 13:25

Important Passages

The many subjects in Hebrews seem endless. One key passage we should read over and over is on *faith* in 11:1-12:2.

If studying the New Testament in topical order,
go now to James.

JAMES

Faith and Works

Setting

James may have been the first New Testament book to be written. It shows the kind of message that God wanted his people to hear soon after Jesus went up to heaven.

The Bible speaks mainly on two themes: the way to God, and the walk with God. No person can walk or live day by day with God who has not first returned to God. Much of the New Testament teaches the way to God—it is by God's grace, through faith in Jesus Christ (Ephesians 2:8). James tells Christians about their walk with God. They are saved , but their faith must bring forth works. A faith that doesn't do that is "useless" (2:20), and a "faith without deeds is dead" (2:26).

James wrote with authority. The letter has sharp and pointed truths. But James' strong words were blended with warmth and love, because he knew his readers were going through hard times of persecution and suffering.

Author
The writer was James, a brother of Jesus, who became a believer soon after Jesus' death (see Acts 1:14; 1 Corinthians 15:7). He was fellowshiping with the Christians at Jerusalem, and succeeded Peter as their leader.

First Readers
James wrote to Jewish Christians "scattered among the nations" (1:1), suffering for their faith in Jesus Christ.

Date Written
Around A.D. 45-50.

Purposes
The many different subjects in this letter show that James had several reasons for writing, including these: to encourage Christians who were being persecuted, to correct wrong teachings or beliefs, to teach right Christian behavior.

Theme
Good works grow out of a faith that is real.

Key Words
Faith, deeds, do, judge, tongue, brothers.

Outline
Faith for Living
Greeting 1:1
   A. Faith in testings 1:2-18
   B. Faith at work 1:19-4:12
   C. Faith not at work 4:13-5:12
   D. Faith in our fellowship 5:13-20

Key Verse
"As the body without the spirit is dead, so faith without deeds is dead" (2:26).

STUDYING THE TEXT OF JAMES

Scanning
Page through the letter, observing the opening lines of each

paragraph. Notice the words "my dear brothers" or "my brothers" are repeated often. This tells us much about James and the readers. Now read the letter in one sitting.

Beginning and End

The opening verse is a short greeting (1:1), and there is no formal conclusion. James used most of the space on his scroll for his main message.

Overview

It is very difficult to see a clear pattern in the things James wrote from paragraph to paragraph. The outline on the preceding page focuses on the subject of *faith*. Below is another way to look at James with *works* as the focus. It is clear that this letter tells about the union of faith and works in the life of a Christian. As we read each paragraph of the letter, we should try to identify its connection with each outline.

JAMES: FAITH AND WORKS

	FAITH IN TESTINGS	FAITH AT WORK	FAITH AND THE FUTURE	FAITH AND OUR FELLOWSHIP	
SALUTATION 1:1	motives for works	the place of works	judgment of works	outreach of works	
	1:2	1:19	4:13	5:13	5:20

Works in the Christian's Life

Motives for Works (1:2-18). "Blessed is the man who perseveres under trial" (1:12).

Importance of Works (1:19-4:12). James gives several key essays about faith and works here. For example:

Deeds (2:14-26). "[Abraham's] faith and his actions were working together" (2:22).

Feelings (4:1-12). "What causes fights and quarrels among you? Don't they come from your desires that battle within you?" (4:1).

Judgment of Works (4:13-5:12). "Your gold and silver are corroded" (5:3).

Ministry of Works (5:13-20). "The prayer of a righteous man is powerful and effective" (5:16).

Important Passages

The testing of our faith with many troubles	1:1-18
The kind of faith that saves	2:14-26
Controlling the tongue	3:1-12
Living peacefully with each other	3:13-4:12

Paul teaches in Romans 4:5 that a person cannot do any work that will make him right with God. Yet James wrote that Abraham was "considered righteous for what he did," that is, his works (2:21). How can Paul and James both be right?

A Bible scholar tells us: "Paul is looking at the root; James is looking at the fruit. Paul is talking about the beginning of the Christian life; James is talking about its continuance and consummation. With Paul, the works he renounces precede faith and are dead works. With James, the faith he renounces is apart from works and is a dead faith" (D.A. Hayes, "The Epistle of James," in *The International Standard Bible Encyclopedia, 3:1566).*

*If studying the New Testament in topical order,
go now to Luke.*

1 PETER

Trials, Holy Living, and the Lord's Coming

Setting

In the year A.D. 64 Emperor Nero decided to wipe out Christianity. Everyone knew about those killed in Rome. Would the fires spread to the Christians in northern Asia Minor? Many of these believers had left their homes in Jerusalem (1:6,7). Now, in a foreign land, they were suffering difficult times, especially from unbelievers living around them (2:11,12).

Things were sure to get worse. Peter did not write this letter to tell the Christians that persecution would not touch them. Instead, he encouraged them to stand true and endure the suffering for Christ's sake and with his strength, no matter how bad the persecution would get. Just thirty years later, when John wrote Revelation, harsh persecution came to these Christians in Asia Minor.

Author

The Apostle Peter (1:1), respected leader of the early Christians

in Jerusalem (5:1) and one of the twelve disciples of Jesus, wrote
this letter.

First Readers
They were Christians, many of them natives of Judah, now living in northern Asia Minor (1:1). They were driven from their
homes because of their Christian faith (see Acts 8:2-4).

Date Written
A.D. 64.

Purpose
Peter wrote to encourage the people to endure hard times, live
godly lives, and look for the Lord's return.

Theme
God's chosen people are known by their holy living and hope
in the midst of a very unfriendly world. Their hope looks to
Christ's second coming.

Key Words
Suffer, troubles, holy, hope, glory.

Outline
Hard Times, Holy Living, and Lord's Coming
Introduction 1:1,2
  A. Hard times and salvation 1:3-12
  B. Life of holiness 1:13-25
  C. God's chosen people 2:1-10
  D. Life of submission 2:11-3:12
  E. Hard times and glory 3:13-5:11
Conclusion 5:12-14

Key Verses
*"The end of all things is near. Therefore be clear minded and self-
controlled so that you can pray. Above all, love each other deeply,
because love covers over a multitude of sins" (1 Peter 4:7,8).*

STUDYING THE TEXT OF 1 PETER

Length of Book
Peter called this a short letter (see 5:12). It is short to him because there is so much more he would like to have said. It is easy to read this letter in one sitting.

Beginning and End
Peter began at a very high point. Between the greeting (1:1) and blessing (1:2) are three phrases that show the work of the three Persons of the Godhead in the salvation of a sinner. We should think about these great, wonderful truths again and again. The end of the letter (5:12-14) is warm and inspiring: "I have written to you briefly, encouraging you and testifying that this is the true grace of God" (5:12).

Overview
Remember the phrase "God's elect" in the greeting (1:1)? A variation of that phrase appears at 2:9. When we read the whole paragraph of 2:9,10, we can see that it is an important message for all Christians. In fact, the entire segment of 2:1-10 gives us the central theme of the letter: *God's chosen people.*

When we read the segments on each side of this central theme (1:13-25 and 2:11-3:12) we see that both are about how God's chosen people should live. Then when we read the two outermost segments (1:3-12 and 3:13-5:11), we observe that both are about the Christian's view of hard times.

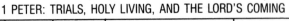

1 PETER: TRIALS, HOLY LIVING, AND THE LORD'S COMING

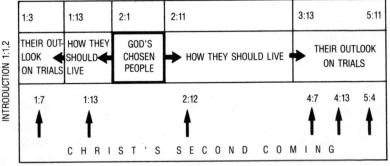

Other Emphases

Christ's second coming. Read the letter again, and look for references to Christ's second coming. There are six in the letter. Peter must have wanted to point out strongly this wonderful truth.

God's chosen people. When we bring all of the subjects of this letter together, we may state the letter's theme this way—God's chosen people are known by the way they keep going without giving up in hard times, by their holy living and by their hope for the Lord's return. Here are several examples of these subjects:

Trials	"all kinds of trials" (1:6)
	"painful trial you are suffering" (4:12)
Holy Living	"be holy in all you do" (1:15)
	"abstain from sinful desires" (2:11)
Second Coming	"when the Chief Shepherd appears,
	you will receive a crown of glory" (5:4).

A very good study to make now is to read the verses before and after each of the six references to Christ's return and see how our hope for his coming should affect our daily lives.

If studying the New Testament in topical order,
go now to 2 Peter.

2 PETER

True and False Prophecy

Setting

About three years after Peter wrote his first letter he wrote again
to the Christians who had fled to foreign lands. In his first letter, Peter had much to say about the suffering that Christians
faced *outside* their fellowship group. In this second letter, he
wrote mostly about more serious dangers coming from *inside*
the group, especially false teaching and people who turned away
from Jesus. So his purpose in this letter was to show who the
false teachers were, and to teach the Christians what they should
do about those who don't love and serve Jesus anymore.

Author

Peter. "Simon Peter, a servant and apostle of Jesus Christ" (1:1).

First Readers

From 3:1 we see that Christians who received Peter's first letter also received this letter. The greeting suggests that the letter is addressed to others also. "To those who . . . have received

a faith as precious as ours" (1:1).

Date Written
Peter probably wrote this letter from Rome around A.D. 67, not long before he died (1:4).

Purposes
Peter wrote to urge Christian growth (3:1,2), to point out false teaching, and to encourage Christians to be ready for the Lord's return.

Theme
He who knows God should guard himself against the teachings of false teachers and pay attention to the truth of Christ's second coming.

Key Words
Know, remember, try hard, false teachers, punishment, last days.

Outline
True and False Teaching
Greeting 1:1,2
   A. Try hard to grow 1:3-15
   B. Powerful coming of our Lord 1:16-21
   C. Description of false teachers 2:1-22
   D. Judgment Day is coming 3:1-10
   E. Promise of a new heaven and earth 3:11-16
Conclusion 3:17,18

Key Verse
"First of all, you must understand that in the last days scoffers will come, scoffing and following their own evil desires" (2 Peter 3:3).

STUDYING THE TEXT OF 2 PETER

Scanning
Scan the letter quickly, noting its length and the segment headings. Then read the whole letter more slowly, marking the Bible text as you read.

Beginning and End
Peter begins with a short greeting (1:1,2). The last two verses show Peter's purpose in writing and end with a sentence prayer of praise (3:17,18).

Overview
Chapter 2 warns about false teaching. This concern is at the center of Peter's message, surrounded by short paragraphs of true teaching. His words "try hard" surround the large section on true and false teaching.

2 PETER: TRUE AND FALSE PROPHECY

SALUTATION 1:1,2	"TRY HARD" 1:3	PROPHECY			"TRY HARD" 3:11 3:16	CONCLUSION 3:17,18
		TRUE	FALSE	TRUE		
		powerful coming of our Lord 1:16	descriptions and prophecies of doom 2:1	Day of God comes again 3:1		

True Teaching (1:16-21). The important message of the Old Testament prophets was about the "power and coming of our Lord Jesus Christ" (1:16). The prophets' message was "a light shining in a dark place" (1:19). How did the prophets know what to say? The answer is "Men spoke from God as they were carried along by the Holy Spirit" (1:21).

False Prophecy (2:1-22). Four paragraphs about false teachers are written here:

   General Statement (2:1-3). "They will teach secretly things that are wrong" (2:1).

   Warning of Punishment (2:4-10a). "God saved Noah . . . who preached about being right with God . . . and punished the evil cities" (2:5,6).

   Descriptions of Evil People (2:10b-16). "Their desire for sin is never satisfied" (2:14).

Destiny of Evil People (2:17-22). "A place in the blackest darkness has been kept for them" (2:17).

True Teaching (3:1-10). Here is the most powerful message of Peter, that on the day the Lord comes again, "The heavens will disappear with a roar, the elements will be destroyed by fire, and the earth and everything in it will be laid bare" (3:10). This is the end of the physical world.

Final Appeal
Read 3:11-16. How did Peter help his readers respond to that prophecy about the *end of the world?* Verses like these should warn every reader: "Since everything will be destroyed in this way, what kind of people ought you to be? You ought to live holy and godly lives as you look forward to the day of God and speed its coming" (3:11,12). "Make every effort to be found spotless, blameless and at peace with him" (3:14).

The phrase "make every effort" sends us back to the opening section of the letter (1:3-15), where we first read these words: "Be all the more eager to make your calling and election sure" (1:10). We learn from this that Jesus' "power has given us everything we need for life and godliness" (1:3).

Important Passages
the knowledge of God	1:1-11
true and false teaching	1:12-3:10
end of the physical world	3:7-10

If studying the New Testament in topical order,
go now to Jude.

1 JOHN

Fellowship With God and His Children

Setting
One of the things Christians will be doing in heaven is
fellowshiping with God and with his people. So it shouldn't surprise us to find that one of the last New Testament books to be
written talks about this happy relationship. That book is John's
first letter.

John wrote the fourth Gospel to teach saving faith in Jesus
Christ (John 20:31) and he wrote 1 John to show believers that
they can know that they have eternal life (1 John 5:13).

Author
The author was John, a fisherman, and "the disciple Jesus loved"
(see John 20:2). He also wrote two other letters, as well as the
fourth Gospel and Revelation. John is sometimes known as the
apostle of love. His tender concern for other Christians is seen
in his letters, where he often calls his readers "my dear children"
and "my dear friends."

John spent most of the last years of his life around Ephesus where he was teaching, preaching and writing. When he was very old, he was taken captive and sent to live on an island called Patmos.

First Readers
They were probably a church or group of churches in Asia Minor who knew the apostle well. Probably they had been believers for a long time. (See 2:7,18,27;3:11).

Date Written
A.D. 85-90.

Purposes
John wrote to strengthen Christians in their faith, urge them to love one another, and warn them about worldly activities and false teachers.

Theme
Christians can know they have Christ as Savior, and they can enjoy fellowship with God and with each other.

Key Words
Know, believe, love, light, children, fellowship, Father, Son.

Outline
Fellowship With God and His Children
    A. Persons of the fellowship 1:1-4
    B. Light of the fellowship 1:5-2:29
    C. Love of the fellowship 3:1-4:21
    D. Way to the fellowship 5:1-12
    E. Certainty of the fellowship 5:13-21

Key Verses
"God is light; in him there is no darkness at all" (1:5). "Dear friends, let us love one another, ... " (4:7). "I write these things ... that you may know that you have eternal life" (5:13).

STUDYING THE TEXT OF 1 JOHN

As we read the text of this letter, it doesn't take us long to learn what an important message John was sharing with his Christian friends. Here are three examples of that message: "God is light" (1:5), "God is love" (4:8), and "If we walk in the light, as he is in the light, we have fellowship with one another, and the blood of Jesus, his Son, purifies us from every sin" (1:7).

Scanning
When we scan the whole letter, we should keep in mind that God is light and love. The book is quite short (5 chapters), yet much longer than John's other two letters.

Beginning and End
There is no formal greeting or conclusion. The use of "we" in the first paragraph may point to more than one writer, or the author might be saying "we" as a way of talking about himself. Before long John begins to say "My dear children" (2:1).

Overview
Throughout the verses of 1 John the theme of fellowship recurs. The main part of the letter, 1:5 to 4:21, centers on the two key statements *God is light* and *God is love.*

1 JOHN: FELLOWSHIP WITH GOD AND HIS CHILDREN

"fellowship"	GOD IS LIGHT	GOD IS LOVE	"believe"	"know"	
PERSONS OF THE FELLOWSHIP	LIGHT OF FELLOWSHIP	LOVE OF FELLOWSHIP	WAY TO FELLOWSHIP	CERTAINTY OF FELLOWSHIP	
1:1	1:5	3:1	5:1	5:13	5:21

First Part (1:1-4) is exciting. The repeated word "life" shows what we all really want. The word "fellowship" with God and with his people comes as a result of that life. We leave the paragraph with this happy note ringing in our ears: "We write this to make our joy complete" (1:4).

Second Part (1:5-2:29) begins on a high peak—"God is light"—

then John leads us down a trail to darker truths. We must put "God is light" next to all of these: "Don't sin" (2:1-6), "He lives in darkness" (2:7-14), "Do not love the world" (2:15), "Many enemies of Christ" (2:18-29).

Third Part (3:1-4:21) We reach a turning point in the letter, and things begin to look better. We are God's children (3:1-3) therefore we do not practice sinning (3:4-12); rather, we love one another (3:13-24) and resist the antichrist (4:1-6). God is love, and whoever loves God must also love his brother (4:7-21).

Fourth Part (5:1-12) John shows that believing in Jesus is the way to this fellowship. And in this final part (5:13-21) he ends the letter by telling about eternal, never-ending life for all believers. You can "know that you have eternal life" (5:13), because "we are in him who is true—even in his Son Jesus Christ" (5:20).

If studying the New Testament in topical order,
go now to 2 John.

2 JOHN

Truth and the Christian

Setting
John's second and third letters help us picture typical local churches during New Testament times. There was a strong, growing faith among the Christians, but the people had their problems. They were the same kinds of problems churches have today! So we can learn much from these short letters.

Author
John the Apostle. He calls himself "the elder" (1).

First Readers
John wrote "to the chosen lady, and her children" (1). The lady was probably a Christian friend of John's.

Date Written
Around A.D. 90, from the city of Ephesus.

Purpose
John told the woman and her family to walk and live in the ways
of God's truth and to beware of false teachers. "If anyone comes
to you and does not bring this teaching, do not take him into
your house or welcome him" (10).

Theme
Christians must love, walk, and live in God's truth.

Key Words
Truth, love, command, teaching of Christ, continue to follow.

Key Verse
*"Whoever continues in the teaching has both the Father and the
Son" (9).*

STUDYING THE TEXT OF 2 JOHN

Length of Book
Because the apostle had limited space to write what he wanted
to say, the things he did write about must have been important
to him.

Beginning and End
The opening lines (1-3) show a greeting, words of love and a blessing. The ending (12,13) is mainly a personal greeting.

Overview
As you'll see in reading this letter, the main subject is truth.

2 JOHN: TRUTH AND THE CHRISTIAN

SALUTATION	COMMAND	WARNING	"GOODBYE"
LOVING IN TRUTH	WALKING IN TRUTH	ABIDING IN TRUTH	JOY
	fellowship ➝ separation		
1	4	7	12 13

Loving in Truth (1-3). "Truth and love" (3) cannot be separated. We can learn much from the letter about living in fellowship with other Christians, that is, loving and enjoying each other and growing together in the teachings of Christ.

Walking in Truth (4-6). We must walk in "the truth" (4) which includes "walking in love" (6). These verses expand on verses 1-3.

Abiding in Truth (7-11). John shows the difference between false teaching and the "teaching of Christ." Christians must follow only the teaching of Christ (9).

"Good-bye" (12,13). John reminds us that joy is a result of our fellowship.

*If studying the New Testament in topical order,
go now to 3 John.*

3 JOHN

Soul and Body Doing Well

Setting
The local church is important in the third letter of John, as it is in the second letter of John. If we keep this in mind as we read the letter, we'll be able to apply what he says to our churches today.

Author
The Apostle John (1:1), respected leader of the early Christians in Jerusalem (5:1) and one of the twelve disciples of Jesus, wrote this letter.

First Readers
This third letter was addressed to a man named Gaius, where the second letter was addressed to a woman (or to a particular church). Gaius was a friend of John's, probably a member of the local church mentioned in verses 9 and 10.

Date Written
Around A.D. 90.

Purpose
The reason John wrote this letter was that Diotrephes, who wanted to lead the church, had rejected the gospel messages John had sent to the church (9,10). John wrote to encourage Gaius and to warn him about evil men like Diotrephes.

Theme
Having a healthy soul and body means following truth, helping others and doing good.

Key Words
Truth, walk, good, help, evil.

Outline
Soul and Body Doing Well
Greeting 1
   A. Report of following the truth 2-4
   B. Praise for helping the brothers 5-8
   C. Warning to reject evil and do good 9-12
Conclusion 13-15

STUDYING THE TEXT OF 3 JOHN

Length of Book
This letter is the shortest book of the Bible, but its message is as important as that of the longest books.

Overview
The theme of this letter is, "Soul and body doing well." We get this from verse 2, "I pray that you may enjoy good health and that all may go well with you, even as your soul is getting along well."

3 JOHN: SOUL AND BODY DOING WELL

	reports	commendations	exhortations	
SALUTATION-1	FOLLOWING THE WAY OF TRUTH	HELPING THE BRETHREN	REJECTING EVIL AND DOING GOOD	CONCLUSION 13-15
	2	5	9 12	

Following the Way of Truth (2-4). "It gave me great joy to have some brothers come and tell about your faithfulness to the truth and how you continue to walk in the truth" (3). As he wrote this, John was surely recalling how Jesus said, "I am the way and the truth and the life" (John 14:6).

Helping the Brethren (5-8). The key repeated word is *good.* "Do not imitate what is evil but what is good" (11).

If studying the New Testament in topical order,
go now to 1 Thessalonians.

JUDE

Keeping Yourselves in God's Love

Setting
Jude's letter strongly urges Christians to be very careful not to
be spiritually poisoned by evil people. There were false teachers
and immoral persons who were secretly entering the Christian
gatherings (4), and Jude, led by the Spirit of God, wrote this letter to warn his friends about that serious danger.

Author
"Jude, a servant of Jesus Christ, and a brother of James" (1).
This was probably the Jude (Judas) of Matthew 13:55, and so
he and James were half-brothers of Jesus. Jude did not consider
himself an apostle but rather a servant of Jesus Christ (see verses
1 and 17).

First Readers
Jude wrote the letter himself to "those who have been called
. . . by God" (1). The only personal words in the letter are the
repeated words, "Dear friends." The friends were probably

members of churches in Palestine or Asia Minor where Jude was ministering at that time.

Date Written
The letter was written around A.D. 67-68, shortly before the fall of Jerusalem (A.D. 70). Peter's second letter, which is somewhat like Jude, was written at about the same time (see 2 Peter 2 and Jude 5-18).

Purpose
Jude wrote to warn Christians against false teachers and those who turned against Jesus. He warned them to keep strong in the faith and to fight against wrong teaching. The evil which was spreading through the churches included immorality, rejection of God's commandments, rejection of Jesus Christ as Savior and Lord, and the mockery of holy things.

Theme
Christians need to be strong in faith and fight for the truth and against false teaching in the church.

Key Words
Dear friends, encourage, remind or remember, evil things, punish, faith, kept safe.

Outline
Keep Yourselves in God's Love
Greeting 1,2
  A. Encouragement to fight for the faith 3,4
  B. Warnings about evil people 5-16
  C. Practical advice for standing strong 17-23
Doxology or Praise 24,25

Key Verse
"To him who is able to keep you from falling and to present you before his glorious presence without fault and with great joy" (24).

STUDYING THE TEXT OF JUDE

Scanning
First, notice the paragraph divisions as they appear on the chart

below. Then read the letter for first impressions.

Beginning and End

Jude began the letter quickly with a short greeting (1,2). His forceful message continues right up to the end, which is a strong word of praise to God (24,25).

Overview

Most of the letter is about the evil people and their sins. The middle section of the letter (5-16) mainly gives Jude's *warnings*. In contrast to the sinful ways of evil people, God's truth stands out with brightness and beauty, like the phrase in verse 21 which is shown as the title: "Keep yourselves in God's love."

GREETING 1,2	ENCOURAGEMENT	WARNINGS ABOUT EVIL PEOPLE			ADVICE	PRAISE TO GOD 24,25
	"Fight hard for the faith."	PUNISHMENT IN THE PAST	DESCRIPTION OF EVIL PEOPLE	JUDGMENT IS COMING	"Build yourselves up"	
	3	5	8	14	17	

Greeting (1,2). Jude gave his friends these assuring words: "To those who have been called, who are loved by God the Father and kept by Jesus Christ" (1).

Encouragement (3,4). Jude gave powerful reasons to obey the command "contend for the faith" (3). God gave this faith (3), but these evil people "are godless men, who change the grace of our God into a license for immorality and deny Jesus Christ our only Sovereign and Lord" (4).

Punishment in the Past (5-7). Old Testament history shows that God was always right in his judgments: he saved his people, but he punished those who did not believe in him and did evil.

Description of Evil People (8-13). Jude used sharp words to show what sin really is: pollute, slander, unreasoning animals, blemishes, shame. "Blackest darkness has been reserved forever" for sinners (13).

Judgment Is Coming (14-16). The Lord is coming "to judge everyone, and to convict all the ungodly" (15).

Advice (17-23). Jude gave much valuable advice to the believers: "build yourselves up" in your faith (20), "keep yourselves in God's love" (21), "wait for . . . eternal life" (21), "be merciful" (22), and hate sin (23).

Praise to God (24,25). "To the only God our Savior be glory, majesty, power and authority, through Jesus Christ our Lord, before all ages, now and forevermore! Amen" (25). Jude wrote with a spirit of great praise to the one and only God, who makes us strong and keeps us from falling.

*If studying the New Testament in topical order,
go now to Revelation.*

REVELATION

Christ Will Win Over Evil

Setting

Can the human race destroy itself? What will happen in the final years of this world's history? God is the only one with answers to such questions about the future. Many of those answers are in Revelation, an important book. It tells about judgments and blessings of the future—mainly those of the last times. Its final chapters point to final destinies: in an eternal lake of fire called hell, or in the eternal New Jerusalem called heaven.

Author

The Apostle John wrote Revelation while he was held prisoner on the island of Patmos (1:1,9-11). This is the last book John wrote, however the real author is God. "It is a message from God" (see 1:2b).

First Readers

John sent the scroll to seven churches in western Asia Minor.

Their spiritual needs were different, but all of them needed to hear the message.

Date Written
John wrote this book around A.D. 95.

Purpose
The book of Revelation encouraged Christians to stand firm under stress of persecution; warned them against turning away from Jesus; and called them to be faithful to Christ. The book gives a loud and clear warning to unbelievers about God's judgment for sin.

Theme
Revelation shows who Jesus Christ is and what his work is now and in the future. It shows Jesus as head over the church, judge and rewarder of the future, and the one who will welcome faithful believers to heaven forever and ever.

Key Words
Two key repeated words are lamb (twenty-nine times) and throne (forty-four times). This lamb is Jesus. The slain Jesus is a measure of God's wrath for sin.

Outline
Revelation
Introduction 1:1-11
    A. Letters to seven churches and songs of praise 1:12-5:14
    B. The future judgments of God 6:1-20:15
    C. The New Jerusalem 21:1-22:11
Closing 22:12-21

Key Verse
"Look, he is coming with the clouds, and every eye will see him, even those who pierced him; all the peoples of the earth will mourn because of him. So shall it be! Amen"(Revelation 1:7).

STUDYING THE TEXT OF REVELATION

Hints   Give attention to the text before you try to understand the meaning.

Focus on the *main* and *clear* passages. These are the important ones.

Look for the reason something is said. For example, if there is a judgment, look for the cause.

Try to discover whether a word or phrase is picture language or something that is actually happening.

If something is hard to understand, look to see what it shows about God or Christ or the Holy Spirit—or even about people and sin. These important subjects are usually clear in the text.

Try to find basic truths in the passage that can be applied to the present day as well as to the time when they were written, such as "I reap what I sow."

Length of Book
Revelation is a long book, and we may wonder why there are so many chapters about judgments (6-20). One answer is that this shows God's great displeasure and anger over sin.

Beginning and End
Words in the opening part (1:1-8) are heard in the closing (22:12-21), such as the words of Jesus, "I am coming soon."

Overview
There are three main parts to Revelation.

THE REVELATION OF JESUS CHRIST

CHRISTIANITY TODAY - Church -	JUDGMENTS TOMORROW - World -	GLORY FOREVER - New Jerusalem -
LETTERS AND SONGS	SEALS - TRUMPETS - BOWLS	NEW HEAVEN AND NEW EARTH
1 setting	6 conflicts	21 victory 22

Christianity Today (1:1-5:14). The seven letters of chapters 2 and 3 are about seven churches of John's time. But they also describe churches of today—the "now" of 1:19. The description of those churches shows how some Christians are living today.

Judgments Tomorrow (6:1-20:15). In Revelation we can watch the judgments of God fall upon the earth with great power: seven seals, seven angels, seven trumpets, and seven bowls. The section ends with the world's last judgments (20:7-15). The last word in this section is "fire." We can learn from these judgments that God and his Son have complete control of world history, that they judge and punish unbelievers and that they protect the people of God, those who remain faithful to the end.

Glory Forever (21:1-22:21). Now we've arrived at the highest point of John's vision, and it is a happy, wonderful climax. Words like "new" and "coming soon" create a mood of joy and excitement. The "new Jerusalem" (21:2) points to heaven as being a huge community of joyful saints living with God and his Son forever. Human words can only *suggest* what heaven is like. But we know that heaven is as sure as the Lord's words, "Write this down, for these words are trustworthy and true" (21:5).

KEY NEW TESTAMENT PASSAGES

World's Physical Dissolution. . . . **2 Peter 3:7-10**

Fellowship . . . . **1 John 1:1—2:2**
Antichrists 2:18-29

Letters to Seven Churches. . . . . . **Revelation 2:1—3:22**
Final Judgment. . . . . 19:1—20:15
Eternal State: New Jerusalem. . . 21:1—22:5

THE MIRACLES OF JESUS CHRIST

Jesus' miracles were superhuman, all-powerful acts and deeds that were evidences and proofs that he was God and Savior, as he claimed to be. The writer of Hebrews says that Jesus' message of how to be saved is proved true by God's using "signs, wonders, and various miracles" (Hebrews 2:3,4). Peter said on Pentecost Day, after Jesus' ascension to heaven, that "Jesus of Nazareth was a man accredited by God to you by miracles, wonders and signs, which God did among you through him" (Acts 2:22).

Many of the miracles that Jesus performed in the first century are recorded in the Gospel accounts. John, author of the fourth Gospel, tells the reader that he reported these miracles so "that you may believe that Jesus is the Christ, the Son of God, and that by believing you may have life in his name"(John 20:30,31).

The grand miracle of the Gospels is the bodily resurrection of Jesus from the grave (Matthew 28:1-10; Mark 16:1-7; Luke 24:1-12; John 20:1-18). The triumphant words of that event are,

"He is not here—he is risen!" And the message to the world is, "Listen to what he says, and believe him to be saved!"

MIRACLES OF PHYSICAL HEALING (revealing, among other traits, Jesus' compassion)

Casting Out an Evil Spirit..............Luke 4:33-35
Nobleman's Son.......................John 4:46-53
A Leper (Skin Disease)................Matthew 8:2-4
Roman Officer's Servant..............Matthew 8:5-13
Peter's Mother-in-law................Matthew 8:14-15
The Sick at Evening..................Matthew 8:16
Two Men Delivered of Demons........Matthew 8:28-34
A Paralyzed Man......................Matthew 9:2-8
Hemorrhaging (Bleeding) Woman......Matthew 9:20-22
Two Blind Men.......................Matthew 9:27
Mute Man With Demon................Matthew 9:32
Lame Man............................John 5:1-9
A Withered Hand....................Matthew 12:9-13
Blind and Mute Man.....................Luke 11:14
Gentile Woman's Daughter.............Mark 7:24-30
A Deaf Mute.........................Mark 7:31-37
Blind Man at Bethsaida...............Mark 8:22-25
Man Born Blind......................John 9:1-41
Blind Bartimaeus.....................Mark 10:46-52
Rebuking Unclean Spirit..................Luke 9:38
Sick, Bent Woman....................Luke 13:10-13
Dropsy ....Luke 14:2-4
Ten Lepers..........................Luke 17:11-19
Malchus' Severed Ear.................Luke 22:47-51
Sick Man at Bethesda..................John 5:1-18

MIRACLES OF RESURRECTION

Widow's Son..........................Luke 7:11-15
Jairus' Daughter......................Luke 8:41-56
Lazarus of Bethany....................John 11:1-44
GRAND MIRACLE: Jesus' Resurrection...John 20:1-18

MIRACLES IN THE NATURAL REALM

Water to Wine at Cana.................John 2:1-11
Escape From Hostile Crowd.............Luke 4:28-30
Catch of Fish........................Luke 5:1-11
Stilling the Storm....................Luke 8:22-25

THE PARABLES OF JESUS CHRIST

Jesus' favorite method of teaching was by parables. A New Testament parable is the story or picture of an earthly thing, person, event or custom used by Jesus to illustrate a spiritual truth. Someone has called the parable "an earthly story with a heavenly meaning."

Many of Jesus' parables tell about the progress of the gospel in the world, the future of the Jews and the Gentiles, the nature of God's kingdom, and the end of the age.

A parable usually teaches one main truth, even though the illustration is made up of many supporting parts. As you read a parable, try to conclude what the main point is. The paragraphs before and after the parable may be clues to that message, and some parables state directly what the message is (e.g., Matthew 13:36-43).

All the major New Testament parables are listed.   Only one
gospel reference is shown for each parable.

PAUL–CHURCH LEADER, MISSIONARY AND AUTHOR

HIGHLIGHTS OF PAUL'S LIFE

Paul's conversion came at the height of his opposition to the church. Acts 9 reports the experience. How Paul and the Christian church came together in the sovereign design of God is shown in the accompanying diagram.

THREE PHASES OF PAUL'S LIFE

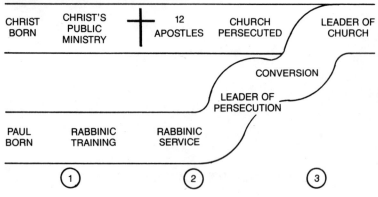

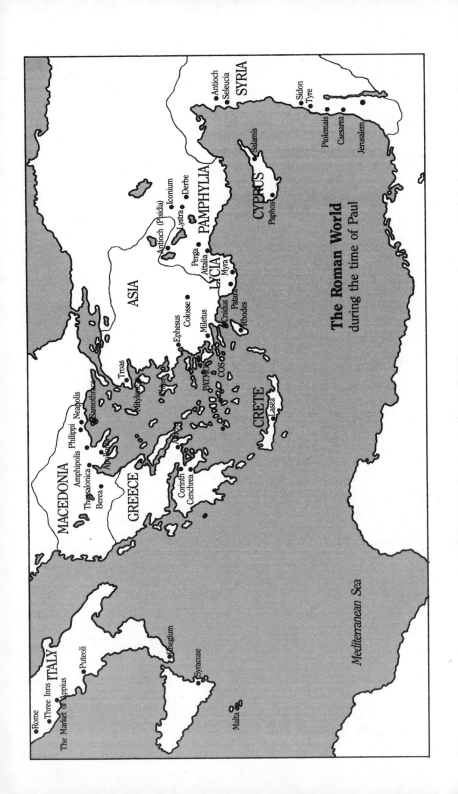

The Roman World during the time of Paul

ITALY
Rome
Three Inns
The Market of Appius
Puteoli
Rhegium
Syracuse
Malta

MACEDONIA
Amphipolis
Thessalonica
Berea
Philippi
Neapolis
Samothrace
Apollonia

GREECE
Corinth
Cenchrea

ASIA
Troas
Assos
Mitylene
Samos
Ephesus
Colosse
Miletus
Antioch (Pisidia)
Iconium
Lystra
Derbe

PAMPHYLIA
Perga
Attalia

LYCIA
Patara
Myra
Cnidus
Rhodes
Coos
Patmos

CRETE
Lasea

CYPRUS
Salamis
Paphos

SYRIA
Antioch
Seleucia
Sidon
Tyre
Ptolemais
Caesarea
Jerusalem

Mediterranean Sea

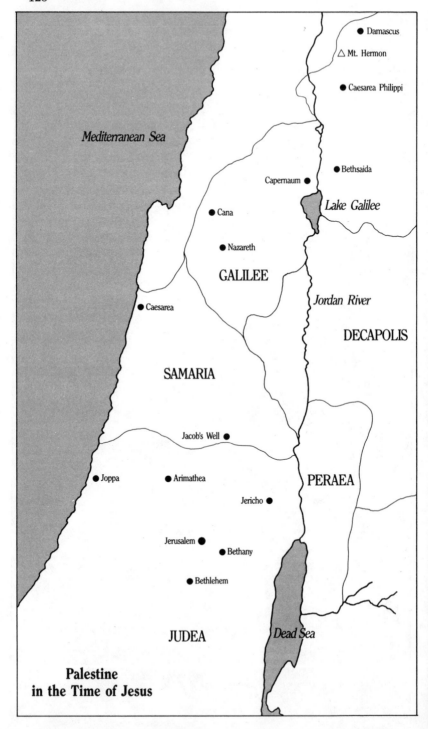

Palestine
in the Time of Jesus